Judaism to Jesus

Finding Love Where I Least Expected It

Simone Sucharov

JUDAISM TO JESUS
Copyright © 2021 by Simone Sucharov

Scriptures taken from the Holy Bible, New International Version®, NIV®. Copyright © 1973, 1978, 1984, 2011 by Biblica, Inc.™ Used by permission of Zondervan. All rights reserved worldwide. www.zondervan.com The "NIV" and "New International Version" are trademarks registered in the United States Patent and Trademark Office by Biblica, Inc.™

Printed in Canada

Print ISBN: 978-1-4866-2107-1
eBook ISBN: 978-1-4866-2108-8

Word Alive Press
119 De Baets Street, Winnipeg, MB R2J 3R9
www.wordalivepress.ca

MIX
Paper from
responsible sources
FSC® C103567

Cataloguing in Publication may be obtained through Library and Archives Canada

To all the people struggling and searching, and to those who have found peace in Jesus the way I have.

Contents

The Old Testament

Section One

Introduction

The beginning is always the most difficult part of a story to tell—
and for me, the most difficult to try to remember. Believe it or not,
I wrote most of this book in a note on my phone. It was easy and
quick to throw down the core moments of my journey, the way
Jesus was introduced to me, and everything thereafter. But if I'm
being completely honest, the memories from before seem faint in
my mind. It only took me a few days to hash out the first edit of
what I call my "New Testament," while my "Old Testament" took
me months.

The purpose of this book is twofold. One, it serves as a personal healing tool that I used in some of my darkest moments. And
two, it serves as an instrument to pursue God's call in my heart to
share my story and reach more people than my inner circle. As this
was a form of healing for me, I also hope it will act as such for anyone who feels personally affected by my choices, but who is also too
afraid to ask questions.

Are they too afraid because they think I'm brainwashed? Maybe. Or maybe they think I was lured into a dark and scary room,
given a presentation, and asked to sign on the dotted line? Naively
committing to something I could never be smart enough to fully

understand? Too afraid because I chose to go against the grain for my own happiness? How dare I! Or maybe they're just afraid that I might actually be onto something that has allowed me to feel true and genuine everlasting happiness.

That sounds about right to me.

I have also written this book for those who don't know me but are walking a similar path. Having the thoughts, let alone taking the actual steps, to proclaim a new faith as your own is a *big* deal, and frightening. To those seeking comfort and refuge here, just know that you are brave for being curious, strong for taking steps of exploration, and in the right hands because God is always there for you, even when others are not. You have the love and support of the Almighty ruler and billions of His followers.

And here, for now, you have me.

Mine is a story that some try to hide, ashamed of a decision that was never truly theirs to feel offense about. God has called me to do a great work in sharing my story with the world, to be vulnerable and raw, going out against my blood religion, my family, and my whole life to share the testimony of how He saved my life. I have poured my heart, soul, and an endless amount of tears into this book. Through writing my story, it was as if I lived these moments again and again, remembering my pain but also strengthening my love for God and the strength He has instilled in me along the way. My story will forever belong to *Him*.

I have spent endless hours praying into each and every word written or sentence structured. I have prayed for soft hearts, open minds, and judgment-free spaces for you. You have picked this book up for a reason, whether that be because you're a family member looking for answers, a personal acquaintance of my new community with Christ, a stranger looking for hope, or an avid reader captivated by my catchy title. You have cracked this spine for a reason. God wants to reveal something to you through my story. Maybe it's as small as a whisper of an uplifting tale to brighten your day, or maybe the point is to turn your world upside-down because you, too, have seen that Jesus is your answer.

Whatever your personal story, whatever baggage you bring to the table, I ask that you leave it behind, open your mind, and remain vulnerable for the rest of your read—because if I'm being honest, no matter how hard-shelled and independent you may be, no one will know.

Here we go...

In the Beginning

Chapter One

V'ahavta et Adonai Elohecha,
B'kol l'vav'cha,
u-v'kol nafshecha,
u-v'kol m'odecha.

Did you sing that? I always do. I can't help it! It's one of the many things drilled into me from my thirteen years of attending Jewish school.

If you have no idea what I'm talking about, no need to worry. This excerpt comes from the Shema, a Hebrew prayer found in Deuteronomy 6:5, Matthew 22:37, and Mark 12:30. The Shema is one of the core, fundamental prayers in Judaism. It is a proclamation of faith and one's devotion to God's Kingdom, and it is recited multiple times a day, specifically in the morning and evening.

If you had asked me three years ago what it meant to be Jewish, I'd have had no idea how to answer. I just *was* Jewish. I had Jewish blood running through my veins and that's all I knew. Today I would answer that question with the above prayer, which translates this way:

Love the Lord your God
with all your heart,
with all your soul
and with all your strength.

But how do you do that, you may ask? Judaism is full of many different ways to connect to God, mainly through prayer, study, and action. Like any other religion, Judaism strives for depth and intimacy with God—God the Father only—and found through upkeeping the commandments, or Mitzvot.[1] Mitzvot are as simple as praying at certain times of day, observing the Sabbath, keeping kosher, lighting candles, and observing holidays.

Judaism is a beautiful and unique religion. And it is God's chosen religion.

⁓

My life was simple. I had an average home with a warm and cozy roof over my head, a "loving" sister to play with, and two parents who loved us and would do anything in their power to protect us. The word *loving* really means that my sister and I would be laughing one minute but then at each other's throats the next. No matter what, my sister and I always ended up sneaking into the other's rooms after dark to play games, because we thought we were the

---

1   The Mitzvoh are a collection of 613 acts found throughout the five books of the Torah.

bosses, unaware that our parents could hear everything and only left us alone because they thought we were cute. We had routine and structure, but we also had a lot of fun.

My mom would tell funny anecdotes of us as toddlers, pouring boxes of cereal out and stomping on them just as she left the room for mere minutes, drawing over the walls with markers or poop, or screaming "HI SISSY!" in each other's faces and giggling hysterically as if we were comic masterminds.

Cute stories, right? It wasn't always this rowdy, though. My sister and I were well-mannered and quiet as young children; we behaved in public and were all right at home, too. There was never much trouble.

The relationships I had growing up with each of my parents were special, the same as anyone else. Quality time was abundant. My mom and I would bond through couch cuddles, shopping sprees, Olive Garden lunches, and plenty of late night gossip sessions. She knew everything and if I wasn't the one telling her, my friends were; she always liked to be in the loop. With my dad, he couldn't care less for the drama or the lunch dates. We bonded differently through many dad/daughter road trips, ski days, going to concerts, or helping with household and school projects. He would read us *Harry Potter* before bed every night, never shy on the British accents, and was always ready to help teach us the things he knew.

I would say I was close with both of my parents in a way unique to each of them, but they had always been there for me when I needed support.

Looking back, it's easy to say that my sister and I were very fortunate to have everything we did. Our basement was a funhouse, a dedicated playroom. We had a dress-up station, board game station,

Barbie station, play structure, and big bins for miscellaneous junk...
the works. The walls were painted with clowns, or flowers, or whatever my mom felt like painting; it was always changing.

The only problem was that we never cleaned up, so as a punishment we had cleaning days. Little did my mom know that our cleaning days were my absolute favourite! I remember waking up with a smile on my face knowing that I could go put on my very special cleaning vest—yes, seven-year-old Simone had a vest *just* for cleaning—and promptly go down to the basement to be "punished" all day long with the joys of putting all my toys away. We weren't allowed to come up until the job was done. Of course we got distracted by playing, but the job always got done. What could be better?

My bedroom was a different story, though. A mess never had a chance to hit the floor because I was always on the ball. It was spotless. Everything had a place and there was order, down to the very angle of my pens on the table. This made it easy for me to realize when someone had been in my room and moved something, which was great for me, but not for the intruder. You could say that organization and order have always been in my blood; I liked having the control.

I was raised in Winnipeg, Manitoba. If you are from Winnipeg, it needs no explanation, but for those who have never been, Winnipeg is the capital of Manitoba, one of Canada's prairie provinces, flat with lots of farming on the outskirts of the Perimeter highway. Freezing cold winters (below -30°) give it the nickname Winterpeg, but there are also incredibly hot summers (above 30°). Winnipeg has a handful of wonderful historic attractions, including The Forks (where the Assiniboine and Red rivers meet, formerly trading grounds in the early 1700s), a rich Indigenous culture, the

4

newly built Canadian Museum of Human Rights, a fantastic culture and arts scene, and my favourite feature: an assortment of beautiful outdoor parks. Winnipeg is known for its abundant and diverse tree canopy, and if you have the luxury of flying over the city in the fall, you don't want to miss the view of luscious green, orange, and yellow treetops out the window!

I was not a girl of many words as a child. Believe it or not, I was incredibly shy. Elementary school was hard for me because of this. My fear of a new friend speaking to me or a teacher calling on me for questions was crippling. I could barely get words out—and if I did, you would be straining yourself to hear what may or may not be coming out of my mouth. Introversion became my middle name as I shyly made my way through school, eating Nutella sandwiches every single day.[2]

I got along just fine with playdates and teamwork at school, but once the bigger events hit—like birthday parties, team sports in gym class, performances on stage, etc.—my nerves kicked in and I froze. These traits definitely developed in me young. I may never have been able to put words to it, or fully understand myself because I was only a child, but I knew I was shy and liked to keep to myself.

This made it difficult for me to make new friends. We went to a private Jewish school, so our grades were small, with twenty to thirty kids maximum. I went through elementary and high school

---

2   This detail doesn't relate much to the rest of the story. I just wanted you to know that, yes, I ate Nutella sandwiches every day for years. Years!

with the same kids. Some cycled in and out, but by the time we got to graduation it was the same core group.

I didn't have an established group of friends until I hit the sixth and seventh grades. It felt great to finally have a group I connected with, which made the next few years easier. But they all eventually left the school, leaving only two of us behind. More than thirteen years later, she and I are still inseparable. Throughout the next few years, we were practically joined at the hip.

I developed a few other friendships through a partnership trip to Israel and ski trips, but I was fairly content with the small and close-knit group I had created for myself.

Since before I can remember, I would wake up every Shabbat morning—the Sabbath, which is Saturday—dress in my nicest clothes, and head over to synagogue with my dad and sister. Once we got there, my dad would get us settled and head over to the opposite side of the *mechitza*, a physical divider established for modesty and focus during prayer time. My sister and I usually went to play next door at the rabbi's house with his wife and children until the service ended and it was time to come back down for *kiddush*, a Shabbat prayer spoken over the wine and bread before lunch.

After the service ended, we would walk with our cousins over to my baba's house for Saturday afternoon lunch.[3] We would run through the door to the strong and spicy aromas of our Moroccan-style[4] meal, a smell that made our mouths water in seconds. My mom, aunt, and baba were usually there with lunch prepared, ready for us to sit and begin to eat. Shabbat lunch always started with *kiddush*, followed by the meal and weekly gossip around the table filled with laughter, eye-rolling, and the occasional disagreement.

Every week, I looked forward to my baba's chicken soup, turkey roll, hard-boiled egg, and her special chocolate chip cookies for dessert. After lunch, my sister, our cousins, and I would go into the back room to find some games to play, which always resulted in the older kids ganging up against us younger ones. Like clockwork, someone always ended up crying.

My saba, a man of very few words, would sit at the head of the table, opening our meal in prayer and laughing along with his broken English jokes or commentary here or there. This was a man who feared God. He was the most righteous man you could imagine, always eager to follow the laws and traditions that tied him so deeply to his faith. Nothing could get in the way of this man and his relationship with God, not even the countless fainting or heart attacks he suffered from adhering to the fasting laws, even against doctor's orders.

---

3   Baba is a term for grandma, saba for grandpa. Baba is a Yiddish term, while saba is Hebrew.

4   My grandparents moved to Canada from Morocco in 1963.

As a young girl, I could never understand the depth of what any of this actually meant, or what it looked like to fear God and hold a relationship with Him above all else. My saba was an inspiration to me and any aspiring person of faith.

And then there was my baba, her spot right across his, the other head of the table with easy access to the kitchen to which she would run back and forth, unable to sit still until everyone else was fed. My baba, the strong neck of the family, has always been ready to fight for what she believes. This is not a woman you want to argue with, but she always had a soft spot for me. She was ready to battle anyone who tried to make fun of me or eat my *special* food. I was an unrealistically picky eater, hence the Nutella sandwich every day, so I always had special food prepared just for me, and how dare anyone try to take my food before I was finished!

We spent our Saturdays this way, from diapers until high school. It wasn't until around age sixteen that I began to protest spending my Saturday in synagogue. My father's side of the family is particularly religious; they keep to all the laws, pray three times a day, and live out the ideal Jewish life in religious devotion. This is uncommon in the modern world of Judaism, as sad as it may seem. Judaism has become a "cultural" religion lacking excitement or knowledge of the laws, traditions, meanings, and origins of the true faith. It's a label with no meaning. Most Jewish families walk through life lighting candles, eating *matzah* (unleavened bread), and singing songs because it's fun, not understanding why they're doing it or what they're saying.

In contrast, you also have a lot of Jewish people who view Judaism as a religion full of obligations and rules. They confuse beautiful acts of faith and belief in God with checking boxes off a list. I'm not sure exactly what the reason for such widespread lack of faith is, but if I had a guess I would say that slowly people stopped seeking interactions with God and over generations they lost sight of what it meant to actually *be* Jewish.

It wasn't long before I blindly found myself falling into the modern Jewish mould. I became bored, disconnected, and uninterested in these traditions. Saturdays slowly turned into no synagogue and just lunch, which eventually turned into nothing for a recent high school graduate with "better" things to do. Shabbat became nothing more than another day of the week where I could sleep in, see my friends, or log extra hours at work.

I worked for a study on health and aging through the local university where we interviewed older adults over the telephone. We asked the participants questions ranging from diet and exercise to relationships, work history, and medical history. The office was always a fun place to be, especially on Saturdays. Our boss didn't come in on Saturdays. I had a handful of coworkers and we were all friends—which isn't to say there was never any drama. We would come in, hang out, snack on our breakfast, laugh, and joke about the ridiculous things participants would say, then update ourselves on all the recent celebrity gossip, boy drama, or life inconveniences. Being at work was always fun.

Some of my strongest memories of Jewish life came from the time I spent visiting our cousins in Montreal at holidays and spending time around the table singing, laughing, and experiencing what an Orthodox Jewish lifestyle looked like. Every law and tradition was kept, down to the pre-ripping of toilet paper, because it was considered work on the Sabbath to rip that day. Back then, none of it was really important to me, but it was always a breath of fresh air to be immersed in that atmosphere for short durations.

⁓

Let's rewind back to age eleven. My sister and I began to prepare for our joint *bat mitzvah*[5]—the rite of passage that marks the coming of age for young Jewish women. We spent hours, weeks, and months practicing our Torah portions, writing speeches, and most importantly searching for the right dress.

Bar/bat mitzvah season overflowed weekend after weekend with synagogue services, receptions, and dance parties for our classmates. It was always the same; prepubescent classmates would giggle and laugh in the synagogue pews, waiting for the service to end, just to run into the reception hall to be the first to snag the chicken fingers, pasta, fries, and ridiculously over-the-top dessert buffet that awaited us on the other side. We could eat as much or as little as we wished because there was hardly any parental supervision. It was a preteen dream.

Following dinner, the deejay would play all the popular party hits, which always included the Macarena, YMCA, Hey Baby, Cha Cha Slide, Cotton Eye Joe, Bohemian Rhapsody, and Hollerback Girl... those were the days! When a slow song came on, the girls snickered and blushed across the room as the boys came over to

---

5   Technically, it was a *b'not mitzvah*, the term used when two women do this together.

request a slow dance. On the dance floor we would awkwardly stand at arm's length, staring in opposite directions, praying that when the music stopped the deejay would come around to give our dance couple a prize.

Oh, to be young and carefree again! That was *the* life. This was as good as it got for the young Jewish community. Most twelve- and thirteen-year-olds hit their Judaic peak during the two years of endless Saturday *bar/bat mitzvah* celebrations. The fun of traditions seemed to fizzle out after that.

Now let's fast-forward to middle and high school, which were full of courses such as Kosher Law, Shoa (Holocaust study), Hebrew language, Tanach (Torah studies), and Jewish History. To say the least, it was jam-packed with the basic Judaic learning needs, focused mostly on the laws and facts, less on what having faith and pursuing God actually looks like. High school was full of great memories, and some not so great, but who doesn't have a few of those? I still never felt like I fit in. I was like a stranger in my own skin, always the shy girl with few friends.

The most I ever felt myself was when I went on my many trips overseas to Israel. To this day, I have travelled there four times. To call it the land of milk and honey is an understatement; Israel is singlehandedly the most beautiful piece of land on this earth, from desert to luscious green, sea to sea, and a cultural community incomparable to anywhere else. This was the place to be.

The first time I visited the country was through a high school exchange program at the end of my Grade Eleven year. We spent seven days working in our partner school in a small town in the north of the country. The strong relationships I built on this trip had me returning again and again for the next three years.

This is where I gained my identity, where I forged my independence and freedom in my young adulthood. I became strong, resilient, and unafraid of anything I might face. Israel was my magical place, my safe space, and my home away from home. My trips were filled with late-night partying, steamy flings, suntanning, and family time whenever I needed to recoup.

Life as an Israeli seemed simple: you go to school, get drafted into the army, and when that's done, only then, you begin your life.

These were my first ventures out into the world, flying alone, navigating a foreign country alone,[6] making myself at home in a new city, finding routine, and most importantly having fun without reporting back to my parents.

Judaism in Israel is on a whole other level. Because it's the predominant religion of the country, it's easy to follow along. Depending on the community you live in, you almost never see a car driving on Shabbat or find someone not observing their rest. Everyone is at synagogue year-round, not only on high holidays. It's almost impossible not to keep kosher because every grocery story, butcher, or convenience store is stocked full.

You're never missing out, because Judaism is just the way of life there. The spirit and energy encompassing the country is so strong that it's impossible not to see the endless possibilities God promised in the Torah. It is tradition to kiss the ground after stepping off the

---

6   Although it helps that I speak the language.

airplane, symbolizing one's appreciation and love of landing in our Holy and Promised Land. The Spirit of God is in the air, everywhere, undeniably for both a believer and not. It is pure magic.

⁓

Growing up was straightforward and easy, for the most part, but something was always off for me. I could never put my finger on what caused me to feel this way, so I carried a lot of anger.

This anger caused me a lot of trouble growing up. It only began to surface in the context of sibling rivalry when I hit my late teens, but once the floodgates opened, the rest was history. I struggled through a lot of fear—of failure, of imperfection, and of loneliness, among others that every angsty teen struggles with. There was an emptiness inside me that I spent what seemed like a lifetime trying to fill.

> It was difficult to realize in the moment that something was missing, but it was.

It was difficult to realize in the moment that something was missing, but it was.

It feels daunting to clearly illustrate what total immersion in the Jewish life in North America looks like. It seems difficult to pinpoint what to share. There was nothing unusual, traumatic, or sad about the way I was raised. I was your stereotypical sheltered Jewish girl who only cared about her looks and the material objects she possessed, because that was all she'd ever known. I went to Jewish school, had only Jewish friends, and was surrounded by Jewish programming outside of school. It was unheard of to think or be different; I was never aware that anything else existed in the world. All I knew was that I would grow up, find a nice man, preferably Jewish, and settle down. That was the way it was done, no questions asked.

This was my life. This was my comfort. This was my *normal*.

Shattered Truths

Chapter Two

Just a few days before my twenty-second birthday, everything I knew to be true—my normal, my entire world—was shattered. My sister found out that my mom and dad had made the decision to separate. Not only did she find out that this was their final decision, but that this had already been going on for years.

My sister came running to tell me, which my parents knew. They never bothered to actually tell me themselves. As soon as the words fell out of her mouth, I felt an instant jolt of heat and anger boil up from the tips of my toes up to my head, and a pit began to grow deep inside my stomach.

> Everything I knew to be true—my normal, my entire world—was shattered.

I made some snide and detached remark about not caring and shooed her from my room. A very typical reaction for me to seem strong, emotionless and detached on the outside, while deeply feeling everything on the inside. And I mean *everything*. What was real anymore? What was the truth and what was a lie? To go from thinking that you live with a completely average and normal family dynamic to finding out in a matter of seconds that you were being lied to and tricked... this felt earth-shattering.

The second my sister left my room, I burst into my infamous silent tears. My mind froze. I felt betrayed and confused.

As the days passed, I wondered why I never got the courtesy of a conversation with either of my parents. This only stirred my already boiling rage.

"It was no one's business," they told us while swearing us to secrecy. "Keep it to yourself until we're ready to tell the world."

Their burden and pain now wrongfully rested on our shoulders, slowly weighing us down, growing heavier and heavier by the minute. The secret was their problem, not mine, yet I felt the substantial pressure anytime we were asked "Where's your mom?" or "Is everything okay?" I had to tiptoe around what language to use in response. The angrier I got, the more I wanted to scream the truth.

Just days after this discovery, I began my bachelor's degree in design. The structure of the program was unlike the average undergrad program. The main weight of the program was focused on a shared studio space, complemented by practical courses all geared to help strengthen the main studio project. In the first year, a heavy amount of time was spent learning the basics of Photoshop, Illustrator, and InDesign, as well as balancing basic hand-drafting, creative work, and public speaking skills. The expectation of excellence, contrasted by only having so many hours in the day, made for a lot of late or sleepless nights, anxiety, depression, and mental breakdowns, not to mention blood, sweat, and tears.

A great example is my very first presentation, or pin-up, which resulted in my professor telling me to "never do that again" in reference to my paper choice.

For those who have heard of this program, or any architecturally related degree, this description of the program doesn't even begin to do it justice or illustrate the high pressure and stress we were under. And this new pressure sat on top of the pre-existing pressure I was already living with at home.

Coming into the degree from a seemingly broken home, I threw myself into the culture. Anything was better than being at home, so I spent as many hours as I could in the studio, obsessing and perfecting my work, just to hang out or be alone. Anything was better than heading home to deal with the chaos there.

When I was home, I would run up and hide in my room to escape and pretend it wasn't real. Every encounter with my parents ended with an explosive argument. Names were called, feelings were hurt, and someone always ended up in tears—usually me, behind my closed bedroom door. Crying myself to sleep became the new normal, but the sadness manifested itself as anger towards the outside world. I preferred to carry my pain alone out of a subconscious fear of what others might say or think about what I thought was an obvious display of weakness.

As we fought, I went as far as asking for our family to seek professional help, like therapy, to at least try and communicate in a healthier way through this mess.

"Your anger isn't *our* problem," they said. "*You* can go to therapy."

It was yet another deflection of the root cause of my pain. It seemed unfair to me that neither of my parents wanted to take responsibility for their choice to inflict so much upheaval in our lives. According to them, it was *my* fault that I was angry, it was *my* fault I felt pain, and therefore it was on *me* to work through it.

I've often found myself stuck in these moral battles, trying to figure out the right thing to do, being the voice of reason, and trying to justify my actions. I would get overly upset when someone wronged me, became irrational, and blatantly disregarded rules. I couldn't understand why my parents couldn't take responsibility where responsibility was due, or even set their own pride aside to do what would be right by me and be open to having discussions or seek professional help. It seemed selfish and childish and quite unhealthy.

Up until this point, I had expressed my anger through hopping into bed with whichever man I was remotely attracted to at the moment, seeking love and comfort the only way I knew how—physically. Even if only for the moment, my brain learned to wire itself through gaining my worth, identity, and love from the number of men who "loved" me for the night.

This particular summer, I spent almost every night with my current fling, running to him for refuge from every fight or feeling that forged its way to the surface. Feeling was *not* acceptable.

But every one of my flings inevitably fizzled, as all lustful relationships eventually do, leaving me alone with myself until I could find the next. I subconsciously found myself seeking what was missing at home: love from someone who would listen to me, hear me, respect me and my words, and be a reliable and dependable source of comfort.

What I could not grasp as a young woman trying to love in a secular world is that when you give up the goods so easily, men rarely care to stick around for the rest. At least those were the men I was finding. "Men" seems like a loose term; you attract what you put out into the world and I definitely wasn't putting out what I truly desired. I constantly left myself heartbroken and more damaged than I'd started out.

You may think it obvious from the outside how destructive and sad my actions were, but I wasn't yet self-aware, mature, or spiritually sound enough to understand the depth of the consequences resulting from my sexual and emotional actions. The physical and emotional ties, the unbreakable bond, created between two people is far too special for one-night stands, flings, and getaways from reality. If there is ever a time to make an argument for why sex should be shared strictly in the covenant of marriage, this would be it. But I won't go there just yet.

The first year of my design program ended off with a big portfolio submission to illustrate my desire to finish the program specializing in either interiors, landscapes, or building architecture.

Ever since I had graduated high school, I had dreamed of becoming an interior designer. The artful organization of a space is something I always enjoyed and it fit very well with my compulsive need for order.

But as we worked through many studio projects in that first year, I learned that, yes, although I love interior spaces, something about landscape design had drawn me in. Silly as it may seem, because I couldn't keep a plant alive for the life of me, I felt a tug on my heart to give something new a try. If it didn't end up working out, I would pursue my master's in interiors afterward.

That portfolio submission led me into the second year of my degree in the landscape stream. This year began with a three-week trip through Europe to study the landscape and city structure of a few major cities including Paris, Amsterdam, and London. Some friends and I had decided to begin our trip two weeks early, travelling first to Iceland and France before meeting up with our classmates. Iceland's landscapes were a fairy tale, with long drives through pastures and mountains, speeding up volcanoes, waterfall after waterfall, natural hot springs, abandoned planes, and city nightlife. This trip was the escape I needed—a couple of weeks of exploring with minimal contact with the people back home.

My friends and I had been in communication with our new professors, Lana and Rob, who would be guiding us through Europe and our first semester of landscape design. They had agreed to send us drawing exercises and assignments to work on while we explored Iceland and arranged where and how we would meet them in Paris. Lana and Rob seemed very professional and kind via email, as none of us had met them before.

To start the trip, my dad drove me to the airport in Winnipeg. First we dropped in to say goodbye to his parents. I remember this day quite clearly. We went in, I said goodbye to my baba, and I was about to go wake my saba, who was asleep in the other room, when my baba yelled at me to leave him alone and let him sleep. Up to this point in time, my saba had been through years of pain and surgery after surgery; he now only lay on the couch calling out in a haze. I insisted again on saying goodbye, only to have her yell at me a second time—and my baba wasn't a woman you wanted to disagree with.

As my dad and I left their house, my heart sank. I felt a deep conviction of guilt for leaving, knowing full well that something bad was going to happen in my absence.

⌐⌐⌐

Arriving in Iceland, my friends and I enjoyed our weeklong visit, followed by a few days between Paris and Nice. Afterward we arrived back in Paris to meet up with our classmates on my twenty-third birthday. We began the class trip by exploring, photographing, and sketching the major parks throughout the city—but then, two days later, I received a phone call from my mom and sister informing me that my saba had been admitted into a palliative care home with an expectancy of mere days, or hours.

My tough exterior crumbled immediately. Alone in my hostel room, I hung up the phone to break down in private, so no one would hear me. I was distraught. Should I stay on this trip that my entire education hinged on, thousands of miles away, or return home to be with my family during this difficult time? I cried for hours, devastated and unsure of what to do.

Death isn't something I had dealt with before, and the amount of pain I felt seemed to outweigh my instinctive need to shove my emotions away. Tears flooded down my face.

The next day, my saba passed away and I remained undecided about where I should be. On the one hand, there was nothing more I could do at home, so I should stay. On the other hand, how could I not be there with my family? How could I spend the next couple of weeks enjoying myself on the trip of a lifetime with this loss hiding in the back of my mind? I knew I would never feel at peace knowing that I missed this funeral and the opportunity to be there and honour his memory.

I spoke privately with my professor Lana. She kindly and comfortingly assured me that whichever decision I made would turn out fine. We also discussed how my grades wouldn't be affected if I chose to return home.

My moral compass kicked in and I decided it was right for me to go home. My sister arranged for my immediate flight to Winnipeg, and after a gruelling day of flying, running to make my connecting flights, and trying to hold back my tears in public, I was home.

Challenge Accepted

Chapter Three

I always saw myself as the rock—the one who kept herself composed and calm on the outside even if she was destroyed on the inside, the one who sat three feet from the coffin at the funeral with a straight face, thinking clearly while everyone else broke down.

I had gotten my tears out before arriving home, tears that wouldn't come again until nearly four years later while I dug up this memory to write about it.

If you haven't yet realized, I never chose to truly feel my emotions. Feelings were shameful and painful and meant for only the deepest of dark moments when I was alone and free from judgment. I'm not sure when that thought developed inside me, but my inner dialogue always told me that my emotions didn't fit with my always-composed and put-together image. Especially tears. Those were the absolute worst sign of weakness.

So I placed my emotions in a box and locked it up with a key to appear strong and independent. You could say that this gave me the appearance of a cold hearted b——, and many would agree, but looking back, this was no way to walk through life... cold, lonely, and afraid to tell anyone what was really in my heart. I thought that vulnerability and rejection was a far greater risk than opening my heart to deep intimacy and friendship.

This was demonstrated in my parents rejecting my emotions. They were the ones who were supposed to accept and love me regardless of how I chose to emote. If I ever had any feelings to show, they appeared in bursts of anger, stemming from all the repressed and pent-up energy I subconsciously longed to release.

Now, this isn't to say that my parents don't love me. I can picture my mom rolling her eyes and defensively scoffing, "Of course I love you." So allow me to clarify something on their behalf. I learned at a young age that when I needed certain types of love and found myself unable to receive them at home, I sought them elsewhere. Home is where stable unconditional love in all forms *should* stem from. When I needed love most, in the form of my parents accepting responsibility for their decisions and being willing to seek professional help alongside me, my feelings were rejected. This left me feeling alienated. I was made to feel that the weight of their problems was my own to carry.

Let me pause for a minute and impart a lesson on love. I'm no expert, but this is what I've come to learn through a hefty amount of soul-searching. Expressions of love can manifest in many forms. For anyone who isn't familiar with it, Gary Chapman's book, *The Five Love Languages*, is a must-read.[7] In it, he explains how the giving and receiving of love is different for every individual but it all revolves

---

7   Gary Chapman, *The Five Love Languages: The Secret to Love that Lasts* (Farmington, MI: Walker Large Print, 2010).

around five love languages: acts of service, quality time, words of affirmation, physical touch, and gifts.

We each have primary receiving languages and primary giving languages. It's important to understand that we can't just love someone the way we might *give* our love best; we also have to recognize how they *receive* love, and do our best to show them love in both of these ways. Through understanding selfless love, we can live out healthy, loving, and secure relationships.

While my parents relentlessly gave love through gifts and acts of service, I needed to receive it through words of affirmation when it came to my feelings and quality time in the form of family therapy. This isn't a dig at either of my parents; we can only give as much as we can understand, and they have always done the best with what they were given.

Thankfully, I have grown and matured over the years to my present understanding of the way love works. To be able to forgive and accept my pain and understand my parents, I can now approach them differently from my mindless, more selfish nineteen-year-old self.

Anyway, moving on.

~~~~~~

My professors, Lana and Rob, had told me to focus on my family during the funeral and *Shiva*, the period of time for mourning death in Jewish culture. However, even though I was told not to worry, I still tried my best to keep up with the drawing exercises and meet up with the group of students who hadn't been able to make it to

Europe. I didn't take kindly to the idea of falling behind and not perfectly mastering the same skills as everyone else.

Upon the return of the rest of the class, our sketchbooks were to be due within a week, just as the first project of our semester was released. I struggled through this two-week project and was obviously behind compared to what the rest of the students were doing, considering that I hadn't received more than a five-minute critique from either Lana or Rob; the others received critiques of ten or twenty minutes.

When it came time to present the project, needless to say it didn't go well. I felt low at this point, not feeling like I was good at something for quite possibly the first time in my life. It triggered the start of my battle with depression. I think depression always ran through me, but my years in the design program surely brought it to the surface and magnified it.

A couple of weeks later, when our grades were returned, I was pulled into my professor's office. Lana looked me in the eye and told me that not only had I failed both my sketchbook and first studio project, but that there was no hope for me to come back from this, pass the course, and move forward in the program. She coldly informed me that my work wasn't up to the standards of the rest of the class and that nobody would want to hire or work with someone like me. I felt my heart sink deep while my pride rose high. But as I sat there in shock, embarrassed, I could barely bring myself to say a word.

I wanted to express my anger. Given the circumstances of what had happened, I felt that I should have been given the leniency and extra help I was promised, which was also the university's policy. I just wanted the opportunity to prove myself.

Indignant, I finally brought myself to speak up. It seemed that Rob and Lana had both forgotten what we'd agreed to. They eventually offered me an extension to rework my sketchbook, giving me another month, which had to be completed on top of the current studio work.

I left the office and ran right to my friend and deskmate, Anna, to tell her what had happened; she was equally shocked and angry. As I talked through my experience with her—leading in anger, as always—I knew I would have to work twice as hard to prove myself and redeem this not-good-enough label I had just been stamped with.

As the rage subsided that evening and the sadness and defeat kicked in, I began to cry. I knew Lana was wrong, but all I could hear were those words—"No one will want to work with you"—repeating over and over again, rooting deeper in my mind each time. The impact of these words, the label she had given me, suddenly became my new truth.

The next morning, I awoke with fresh eyes, having decided that of course I would not drop out of this program I had worked so hard to be a part of. I would work extra hard to prove my professors wrong and pass the semester with flying colours.

In those next few weeks, all the unionized professors at my university went on strike, taking Rob out of the picture and leaving only Lana behind because she was a sessional instructor.

As the days passed, the harder I worked, the more Lana shut me out; I would approach her with new drawings to ask for guidance, only to be turned away. She'd say, "You'll have to figure it out for yourself," leaving me to feel even more alienated and alone.

I worked hard and appeared like my strong usual self on the outside, but inside I felt doubtful, scared, and insecure. Balancing the extra work on top of the already overflowing coursework, with no support from my professor, left me feeling exhausted, overworked, and defeated. I was the first to arrive every day, and one of the last to leave, putting in the extra time to try and prove myself, but none of that seemed to matter. In Lana's eyes, I had already failed.

The day I was to resubmit my sketchbook, I confidently sat down with her, eager to share the few sketches I had perfected, as well as a handful of other drawing exercises I had completed. As she flipped through, barely taking a second to look at my work, I felt my heart sink again.

She handed the book to me and, in disappointment, snarled, "I was expecting more. Your sketchbook should be full."

Devastation overtook me as she repeated the same script she had eagerly come prepared to repeat.

"Your work is not up to standard. Nobody will want to hire you or work with you moving forward. You would never be accepted into any master's program at this rate."

I froze, my mind blank. I was unable to string together more than one word: "Okay."

Lana handed me the letter of recommendation she had already signed, advising me to drop out of the program. She had made up her mind about me long before this moment, long before she had known what I was capable of.

How could a professor, a *teacher*, a *leader*, an *educator*, be so unwilling to teach, lead or educate? Instead of guiding me and providing the extra attention I needed, Lana left me drowning with no life preserver. She didn't do her job.

Her cold, unwelcoming approach to education rubbed many in our class the wrong way, which left little respect in people's hearts for her. However, none of their experiences were to the same extent as mine.

Lana informed me that the team members in my current studio project had already complained about me not being able to keep up. Go figure. Talk about feeling even more rejected. I was balancing an entirely different project on top of what they had been doing, so it wasn't that hard to believe.

There was no sympathy, emotion, or guidance behind her heartless words. She advised me to speak with the faculty advisor about the decision I had to make, assuming they would guide me in giving up.

"Okay," I said again as I got up and made a beeline right for the advisor's office.

I set up an appointment with her as Lana had suggested, not to discuss my voluntary withdrawal from the program, but rather the neglect and abuse I now felt certain I was receiving from my professor.

With disappointment and rage boiling through me, I told the advisor my story and she was in full agreement that the lack of attention I had been given was inappropriate. She recommended I file a formal complaint through the appropriate university channels, which I eventually did.

As the semester went on, I continued to push myself beyond my means to prove Lana wrong. It was apparent that she wasn't impressed that I hadn't respected her recommendation and instead remained in the course. The more I tried, the worse things got. I would present my hours of work, the many pages of research and drawings I had worked on, only to be cut off mid-sentence: "You're not showing me anything. You have done nothing." Then she would walk away.

I would get two minutes of her time when most students got twenty, and eventually she just stopped talking to me altogether. The more I pushed, the less I got until most of the other students finally began to notice the neglect and went out of their way to help me progress and succeed with my projects.

There was one particular day when Lana's purposeful disregard for me pushed me over the edge. Enraged, I sent an email to the head of the department and asked to set up a meeting to discuss some of the things that had been happening. He replied that he already knew of the situation and advised me to speak to Rob, who would be returning from his strike the next week.

I waited the week and tried to discuss what had been going on with Rob, only to have him cut me off and tell me that I was exaggerating and misunderstanding Lana. He said he would take another look at that first studio project to appease me.

Excuse me?

The studio was no longer a safe space for me to hide from my woes. I no longer had a home away from home. I felt insignificant, undervalued, inadequate, and completely abandoned by every single figure of authority in my life. I was endlessly sad, overworked, and tired; there just weren't enough hours in the day to do the amount of work I needed to do.

As time went by, Lana's words cut even deeper. These wounds never seemed to heal. I had been pushed aside, my concerns swept under the rug. I didn't understand why nobody was looking out for me. Why did nobody care? I wasn't paying thousands of dollars to show up at school and be neglected and abused instead of receiving the education and attention I deserved. This was not *right*.

But there was nothing I could do. I was powerless in a sea of arrogant, self-righteous designers who cared more about their reputation than actually doing their jobs as educators and leaders in the design community.

Moving forward, I only dealt with Rob and was no longer in contact with Lana, until the final day of studio rolled around in December and we presented our projects. Lo and behold, I magically passed the term with just one percent higher than the required passing grade. Just enough, no more and no less, to keep me quiet and push me forward in the program. Just enough to sweep the real problem under the rug and not stir up anymore waves for the faculty to deal with.

Or so they thought.

I filed a formal complaint through the university, which changed my letter grade ever so slightly. But the complaint never gained any real traction, seeing as Lana was hired for a full-time position just months later by a committee that *I* sat on, regardless of the accusations and poor term reviews.

Did your university have those silly multiple choice bubble sheets the students were forced to fill out at the end of each semester? The ones with generic questions about a course and multiple choice answers to assesses its structure? Funny story: those don't get used for anything, at all. They don't even get passed along, and if they do, any negative comment, no matter how constructive and true, gets thrown away. I can account for at least three other students who gave all zeros for Lana, and I can promise you these low scores never found their way onto her flawless one hundred percent staff review, which I looked over as the student representative on the hiring committee during her interviewing process.

For the duration of my degree, I constantly felt inadequate and ashamed of the work I produced. Every time I opened my mouth for review, crippling anxiety overtook me, knowing the rejection that awaited me on the other side. Critiques hit me harder because all I could hear was Lana's voice taunting me: "You are not good enough. Nobody will want to work with you. You will never make it." Behind every line I drew, every idea I had, every word I spoke, these comments weighed me down, magnifying my perfectionism to a point that I couldn't move forward with a project until I decided it was *finished*. But sadly nothing ever was.

> I needed a change. I needed something to hold on to. I needed something to save me.

This kept me at a standstill and I never advanced with my coursework. I didn't want to feel stupid, bad at something, not good enough, or a failure ever again. I couldn't let go of my negative thoughts. I couldn't just complete the work necessary to be successful. I constantly stood in someone else's shadow, following their footsteps, unable to complete anything.

University had once been a place where I could express myself, feel safe, and grow. Until I was let down.

I needed a change. I needed something to hold on to. I needed something to save me.

My depression only increased until I finally snapped... but we'll get to that.

The One Who Changed Everything

Chapter Four

Let's rewind a couple of months back to November. I was working at my desk one day when I looked up and felt my heart skip a beat. Standing before me was this brown-haired, brown-eyed, tall and lean, adorable man. Though we had been in the same studio space for months, I couldn't remember ever seeing him before. Something moved in me; a force drew me in. I chalked it up to pure physical attraction, but I continued to feel like there was more to it. Maybe he was the *one*. There was something magnetic about him and I knew I needed to be a part of it.

It was months before Chase and I exchanged any real words. I had a lot going on with Lana and my coursework. I mostly found myself glancing across the studio or classroom, wondering what he was like, wondering why I was so attracted to him and why I felt such a strong pull towards someone I knew nothing about.

I finally scraped together enough courage to message him over winter break. Through "researching" him on Facebook, I learned that he had been in Mexico with his family. This knowledge gave me enough confidence to strike up a conversation. We chatted for two days before the conversation naturally ended and winter term resumed.

I remember the first time we spoke in person. I had been sitting in the student lounge, running through my deck of flashcards for an upcoming exam when Chase came to grab his lunch from the fridge. He asked me how I was doing and what I was studying. When he walked away, my heart almost burst out of my chest. I had barely been able to string a sentence together in response. It was *very* awkward.

During the next few months, it was more of the same—me glancing across the room, being too nervous to make eye contact or start an actual conversation, so insecure and unsure of how to initiate a real relationship with this person I couldn't keep off my mind. This was different than my other "relationships." My intention was not to try and sleep with him; I wanted to *know* him, to really get to know him and see where it might lead.

Finally, as the end of the semester rolled around, I felt a tug in my heart, knowing that my window of opportunity was closing. After graduation, Chase would likely be moving to Calgary where his family lived.

On the night of our year-end exhibition, an evening when students of the faculty displayed their work and invited friends and family to celebrate, I knew I had to make a move. I messaged him and asked if he would be there; he said yes. Anticipating how the night would go, I began to get ready.

After all the effort I put into my outfit, hair, and makeup, he didn't show up, later informing me that he was sick at home.

That was it. I had missed my chance and he was gone forever.

I had been given a free ticket to the graduation dinner and dance the next evening. After going back and forth with myself, thinking about how much I disliked big events but also how much I hoped to see Chase one last time, I decided to go.

For the second night in a row, I dressed up and headed out. Very unlike me.

I arrived to an overjoyed greeting from Anna and spent the night by her side. Almost an hour in, I had one drink, trying to work up the courage to say hi to Chase.

Just as I was about to stand up, I noticed him put on his suit jacket and leave.

He left.

I told myself that it just wasn't meant to be, then had another drink and continued on with my night.

Before I knew it, it was midnight. I hopped in my car—after sobering up, no need to worry—and drove Anna home. As we sat in her bedroom, I shared how I felt and after some late night girl talk, and the slight liquid courage still active inside me, I decided to message Chase and ask why he had left so early. One thing led to another and the next thing I knew I was on my way to his place. As I drove in his direction, half an hour later, I was excited yet unsure of what was about to happen.

It was 1:00 in the morning by the time he and I pulled up at a local park. We talked for hours. It was as if we had known each other forever. The more we talked, the more my heart grew, knowing that everything he was saying, every detail he shared, his personality, his quirks, the way he thought, was the exact reason I had been attracted to him all along.

He was the real deal.

As the hours went by, we had flown through most of the important topics of conversation and decided to end our night with a movie at his place. Just as the movie ended, Chase leaned over and kissed me with a big goofy grin on his face. The moment his lips touched mine, I knew in my heart that I had stumbled upon what was about to become the greatest love story I would ever live.

Little did I know that it wouldn't actually be with him.

We spent the next three days together, joking, laughing, and getting to know each other before, as I had suspected, he moved to Calgary. On our last night together, things escalated when he opened up to me about his Christian faith. He said that he was unsure if he would be willing to maintain a relationship with someone who didn't share that with him.

My heart sank. I had no idea what a Christian even was, or what that meant, but I was sure that the spark we shared could be strong enough to overcome anything.

> The moment his lips touched mine, I knew in my heart that I had stumbled upon what was about to become the greatest love story I would ever live.

We woke up the next day and I watched him pack his bags into his car before coming over to say goodbye. I cried all the way home, thinking about how I had just had the best three days of my life with a guy who had swept me right off my feet. He perfectly fit the mould of the man I had always imagined myself ending up with. But I had no idea if I would ever see him again.

We texted throughout the next week. Everything seemed to be progressing well. But only a few days later, I received the first of many hesitant texts in which he expressed further doubt that he could maintain a romantic relationship with someone who wasn't a Christian. According to him, our morals and values were not the same, and while things were great right now he didn't think it would work out long-term.

As painful as these texts were to receive, I really was unsure of what he was talking about. All of a sudden there were morals and values? What morals and values? I had asked him those questions many times, but he had never given me a clear response. He had never shared his morals and values with me, nor had he ever asked me about mine. How could he make this judgment?

As devastated as I was, I knew this was not the end. How could I finally meet my perfect man and have it end, just like that, in a matter of a week?

Even though Chase claimed he didn't want to be with me, we continued to talk as if that conversation had never happened. We texted, we flirted, and we made plans to see each other again when he was back in town for his convocation in June.

June rolled around and as we sat on a park bench catching up as if no time had passed. Suddenly those same hesitations came up again, but the conversation didn't last long before we ended up back in bed. Confused, I again brought up our differences of faith. To my surprise, Chase seemed to have had a change of mind. It was obvious to me that he felt the same for me as I did for him, but he was torn between this "Christianity" thing that I didn't understand.

The more questions I asked, the less I could get a clear response from him. What did being a Christian actually mean? What did Chase mean when he said we could never get married? Who the heck was this Jesus? And why did people follow Him? He sure seemed like a quack to me.

It seemed that Chase didn't actually know these answers for himself, making it more difficult for me to want to believe or understand him. I really thought the whole thing sounded ridiculous.

After spending the entire week together, Chase returned home, leaving things in a stable place. The weeks went on and we spoke daily, continuing to get to know each other on a deeper level. We didn't talk much about faith, but the issue always seemed to rear its ugly head after a while.

I was Jewish, I would always be Jewish, and there was nothing to discuss. I wouldn't turn my back on my heritage and my family. Chase could love me as I was, and if he truly loved me, this Christian thing wouldn't matter.

He didn't care that my family would disown me, only that his family would disown him. It started to feel as if he didn't respect me because I wasn't like him. It was a mystery to me. The language he used and rationalizations he came up with made no sense. His tune was constantly changing, flipping back and forth. One day he'd tell me he liked me, followed closely by, "But what would my family think because the Bible says…?"

This inevitably led us to take a break.

During this break, I finally decided to seek professional counselling. The weight of everything that had happened with my family, my saba, my crisis at university, and my relationship with Chase had my depression at an all-time high.

I sought out a local Jewish psychologist. As nervous as I was to face my problems, I quickly realized what a benefit therapy was. We began by covering the basics of my family history, slowly moving through my experience with Lana and relationship history.

Chase became a prominent topic during these sessions, as the weight of religion on the relationship felt heavy. I couldn't have been clearer that I wasn't interested in converting for him. We would discuss the pros and cons of dating someone from another faith, and my therapist helped me think through my feelings.

However, looking back, I would say that I was uninterested in hearing anyone say that my relationship with Chase wouldn't work out. I was determined that this was the right relationship for me and that Chase and I would make it work.

One month passed before we spoke again. Chase reached out and we resumed our conversations as if nothing had changed. Talk about confusing! For months, we spoke daily, only this time it had escalated to phone calls that always lasted two or more hours. Chase had become my best friend, and I his. It felt as if nothing could tear us apart, and the closer we got, the more serious things became and the harder it was to engage in conversations about faith.

Our conversations slowly drifted towards the what-ifs. What if we lived in the same city? What if we got married? What if we had kids? What if I became a Christian? He asked me so many times to convert so that we could be together, but each time I firmly stood behind my strong Jewish identity. I knew in my heart that I could never change myself so drastically for anyone, let alone a man, no matter how much I loved him. I knew that my family would turn their backs on me. I would be rejected and disowned. The cost of pursuing my love for him wasn't worth the persecution I could expect from my family.

"If you really want to be with me, you'll do it," Chase would sometimes say. Walk away from my family, he meant.

Floored by this statement, I began to get angry. I couldn't understand why he didn't just accept me for who I was and love me for me. It seemed very clear to me that Chase only cared about the judgment and persecution that would come from his family. For Chase, Christianity was a religion full of obligation, forced upon his life by his parents. He hadn't yet made the faith his own. Similar to how I felt about leaving Judaism, that's how Chase felt about his ties to Christianity.

When his parents finally found out I existed, they disapproved and made his home life quite difficult. There were constant arguments and conversations about how his life was derailing from the path the Lord had for him; they shamed and judged him for the relationship and connection we shared.

What a bunch of quacks, I thought. I couldn't understand why they fought so hard to control Chase and his actions, treating him like a child instead of like an adult capable of making his own decisions.

A bit fed-up, Chase finally booked a plane ticket to come see me just before Christmas so we could spend time together and finally sort this thing out. I began to count down the days.

December 14, 2017 came and I excitedly rushed to the airport to greet Chase as he rode down the escalator. The moment his arms wrapped around me, I felt every inch of my body relax. It felt like home, a feeling I wanted to experience for the rest of my life.

We enjoyed a week full of endless laughing, joking, deep discussions, and "making out." Everything was perfect—

—until it wasn't. We had booked a hotel room for two nights, and on the second night things took a bit of an ugly turn. After returning to our room for the night and climbing into bed, the elusive discussion of faith came up for the last time.

We began to fight. Throughout this trip, I had seen a side of Chase that made me rethink my strong stance. I argued that the love I felt for him was strong enough to overcome our differences. We could raise our kids however he wanted, I would join them for church, and we could make it work. But I still wouldn't change who I was. He cried into my shoulder, saying that he was afraid of what God thought of me. Even worse, he felt sad that I was going to hell.

Chase expressed his love for me in return. He wanted to be with me, but he was also unwilling to budge. He revealed that the purpose of this trip had been to give me this ultimatum and convince me to go to church and change my beliefs, motivated solely by his parents' demands. With every word, he spoke with the fear of having to go home and tell his family that he had failed.

That night, our relationship officially ended. After our last few days together, I drove him back to the airport where we said a tearful goodbye.

The Paradigm Shift

Chapter Five

After Chase left, I drove home and immediately cracked open the Bible he had bought for me. I began reading Matthew.

Why does it keep referring to the Jewish people as hypocrites? I asked myself. I got angry and quickly slammed the book shut.

The next day, and for many after, I continued to try and get through the gospels, each time boiling with anger at the harsh language and accusations coming from this Jesus fellow's mouth towards the Jewish people of His time. What was I even reading? Why did so many books repeat the same story? I was uninterested but determined to see whatever Chase saw in this flimsy and offensive book I had lying in front of me.

My mind was pretty closed off. I was determined to appear as if I was trying when in reality I was only searching for loopholes. I wanted to understand where Chase was coming from, to be what he wanted me to be while still managing to stay who I was. It was a task tougher than anything I had ever taken on, but when a determined Simone decides she is going to do something, nothing can stop her.

As I shared what I was reading with Chase, asking him questions or sending verses I thought were nice, he seemed unemotional and unresponsive with no care for what I was doing. He had given up on me. I asked him questions, asked him to explain or discuss what I was reading, but he was unable to string together enough words to truly engage with me.

This was hard for me to understand. If this was what he actually believed, why was it so difficult for him to share with me? Where was his passion? At my very minimal stage of exploration, I could discuss Christianity at far greater length than he seemed to be able to.

I was trying. I was trying so hard *for* Chase. I wanted him to be happy with me and I wanted things to work out. I longed for his and his parents' approval, a desire that had grown greatly in me over the last six months.

Striving to please others or gain their approval has been a common theme throughout my life, although it was often subconscious. I often found myself wanting to master something just to prove myself worthy. Being the best and being recognized was a satisfying goal, to prove that I *could* be loved, that I *could* have value, that I *was* smart. This wasn't a thought process I was self-aware of, so I can't pinpoint the root cause, but looking back, there are obvious patterns in my behaviour.

What I failed to understand at this point was that there is no perfection without God, no value or wisdom stronger than that which comes from a deep and personal relationship with Him.

The first time I entered a church was early January 2018. My friend Anna had been raised a Christian, and throughout my long battles with Chase she had been my primary source of comfort. When I had finally decided it was time to check out a church, Anna was excited to tag along in support.

As we walked in, I felt my anxiety rise, my chest heavy, heart racing, and very short of breath. It was against the Jewish law to step foot in a place of worship during another faith's service. With this in the back of my head, I feared God was going to punish me or smite me on the spot.

We entered the building and went straight up the stairs to the back row of the balcony, as far back and invisible as we could get. I avoided making eye contact with anyone and kept my eyes glued to the back of Anna's head. I sat on the edge of my seat, anxiously expecting the worst and eagerly ready to run out the door.

The band came on stage and everyone stood, but I remained seated. I wasn't really sure what was going on, so I asked Anna if I should stand. She comforted me in saying I could do whatever felt right.

People began to sing along, closing their eyes, lifting their hands, and swaying from side to side. Sceptical and afraid, I stared at everyone, thinking about how ridiculous they looked. Why was everyone so into the music? This wasn't a concert.

The service elicited a new level of discomfort I hadn't even known existed. I just wanted them to get on with the service, for everyone to sit down and get this show on the road so I could get back home where I was comfortable. Even though I'd been given the rundown of what to expect, I still felt unprepared. Although I would typically feel the need to run in a situation like this, I knew I was committed to being there that day.

The pastor came up and spoke for about thirty minutes about the story of Abraham and Sarah in Genesis.

Hey, I know this story, I thought. My body began to relax as I sank into the chair. He spoke well, mispronouncing a few names, which eased my anxiety a bit. I actually agreed with a lot of the points he made. He didn't even mention Jesus until the very end, which confused me. This was a *church*; weren't they supposed to talk about Jesus? But instead they'd talked about the Torah. These were the same stories I had grown up with. What was going on?

By the end, I could feel my anxieties lifting. My body had calmed as I engaged with the words the pastor spoke. It felt as though he was speaking directly to me, that he somehow knew my situation and had prepared the entire service just for me.

And there was definitely no smiting... I was alive and perfectly fine.

While discussing the experience with Anna on the way home, I tried to rationalize what I had just heard, tried to connect it to my Jewish self. I was unsure if I would ever return to that church. It seemed funny to me that the pastor had made me feel so connected to a story I had heard my whole life but never thought much about.

Until Chase had questioned me about my faith, my spiritual ties had been very faint. But these were the stories of my upbringing, the ones I'd heard in elementary and high school over and over again. To me they seemed ordinary and boring, like fairy tales you tell before bedtime that kids eventually grow out of. They were never special. Being Jewish was always my identity, and I had strongly clung to that when it came into question, but the passion and longing for depth in my religion never truly existed.

My confusion over the sermon I'd heard, and the process of questioning identity, became so overwhelming that I felt scared. But surrounding my fear was a presence of calm and peace, a feeling I couldn't put my finger on because I'd never felt it before.

Over the next two months, I continued to uncomfortably read my Bible, follow up with church sermons online, and go about my life as if that day hadn't been all that special.

⌒

After a serious mid-February fight over my mental health, Chase and I didn't speak in several weeks. I sat and wondered what he was doing. I also began to wonder what a life with Jesus would be like. How might things change if I made this decision? I was in limbo, still only searching for answers and loopholes to regain my closeness with Chase. But I wasn't as opposed to what I was learning as I had thought I would be.

On March 12, 2018, my mental health took a serious turn and I snapped. The stress of the upcoming deadlines at school, lack of sleep, lack of routine, not eating, and the hole in my heart where Chase used to be all became too overwhelming for me to handle.

In a typical bout of sadness I would spend a full day in bed, probably not eating well for a day or so, and then I'd move on. This time, I didn't leave my bed for four days, crying and throwing up the nothingness inside me because I hadn't eaten in almost a week. I lost ten pounds.

What was the point anymore? Why didn't this crisis ever end?

Whenever I felt like nothing mattered, I talked to God, praying and asking Him to take everything away and make the pain stop. These were the only times I spoke to Him or acknowledged that He was real. I had prayed this prayer many times, mostly in the darkest of dark moments, asking God to make things easier by not waking me up in the morning. I never truly had the strength to end my life and I always looked to Him to be the "bad guy," the one I somehow knew had the ability to quite literally smite me dead.

> He answered my prayer for death with life... *His* life.

I can't say that this was ever a conscious realization of talking to God, but it seemed that I knew I could run to Him when I needed help. I wanted my pain to end, but I couldn't see a light at the end of the tunnel. I just wanted to shut off and die.

As usual, I fell asleep the night of March 12 in a nice wet puddle of tears.

But something was different this time. As I slept, something changed inside me. I woke up in the same sad mood as always, but I felt a shift. The thought of ending my life had left my mind. I was less uneasy, and when I picked up the Bible to read it, it felt as if I had a completely new mind.

God had answered my prayers that night, but not in the way I'd asked. I couldn't understand it at the time, or put a description to what had happened, but God doesn't always answer our prayers the way *we* want Him to. He will do what He knows is best, even if we disagree.

God is our author and perfecter (Hebrew 12:2), and so He uses these seemingly hopeless moments to completely change the trajectory of our lives. He answered my prayer for death with life... *His* life. God used Himself to take my pain away, to show me mercy and give me grace. He paved the pathway for me to realize that Jesus had died so that I could *live*, not die also.

The New Testament

Section Two

Open Heart, Open Mind

Chapter Six

That night, changed everything. God met me in that moment and shifted my heart. He surrounded my pain with Himself and His grace. Where I had understood death to be my only option, He saw only His life. Positivity began radiating through me and I wanted to learn more.

Chase and I had talked about me getting in touch with his brother, Brandon, for quite some time. He kept insisting that Brandon would be better able to help me understand Christianity, and I would be able to learn without having to deal with Chase's emotional frustration.

As my heart opened, I decided it was time to reach out and gain clarity and understanding of the Bible. In my handful of conversations with Brandon, I finally began to gain traction and understanding of who Jesus was and what He stood for. It was all starting to make sense. The shift suddenly made room in my heart and mind to understand and relate to the same words that had once made me so angry.

Brandon had a view of life that was unlike anything I had ever heard. He had an answer for everything, stemming from the Bible—and if he didn't, he offered to look it up for the next time we spoke. He was patient and understanding of my opinions and blunt questions and was never offended or angry. I finally began to see that Jesus hadn't been a Jew-hating troublemaker, but rather a peaceful, loving, and gentle man sent to save the Jewish people.

With my new clarity and basic understanding of the Bible, I began to question Chase. I could see the positive, compelling, relentless, and passionate faith his brother possessed, which gave me a small peephole into what being a Christian might actually mean. But this was *not* who Chase was. The peaceful way of life, the time set aside to spend intimately with God in His word or through prayer, the simple words of praise for who Jesus was... these attributes were nowhere to be found in Chase's life.

I was curious to know if Chase thought that way or even saw the world like this. I was drawn to the Jesus Brandon was showing me through our phone conversations. For Brandon, Christianity was a faith full of heart and belief, not obligation—and I began to see the Bible, church, theology, and history behind it all. Chase's brother was a wealth of knowledge and a very important stepping stone leading down my road to Christ.

The following Sunday, March 18, I walked into church and went up the stairs to the back, as I had been doing for the past few weeks, but something was different; nothing blocked me from making eye contact with the people around me. My heart wasn't beating out of my chest and my breath wasn't short.

It was Baptism Sunday and a video came on of a young girl, around my age, sharing the story of her mental health battle, which resulted in her turning to Jesus; it felt as if she was speaking right to me. I could relate. I understood her pain. And as I thought about how much I could use someone like Jesus in my life, a tear fell from my eye. I quickly wiped it away in fear that someone might see me and tried to refocus my attention on the young girl standing in the pool of water; I had no idea what a baptism was. I felt my emotions swell, but I didn't understand why. Why was someone standing in a pool of water making me cry... in public? Everyone cheered, but I just felt embarrassed and confused.

At the end of the service, the pastor announced that the young adult group would be meeting on Tuesday. Why not? I plugged it into my calendar.

On Tuesday, I waltzed in and confidently sat down beside two girls who looked about my age. I introduced myself. Now, keep in mind how out of character this was for a shy and introverted Simone. After we got to talking, they became fascinated by my story and were excited to share in my journey and answer any and every question I asked. I hesitated to share my Jewish background, but once I did they beamed with excitement, telling me how powerful my knowledge of the culture Jesus was raised in was.

The longer we spoke, the more I noticed how they related every answer back to Jesus. This made me uncomfortable at first, but over time I've learned how beautiful it is. Was this what a life of Jesus would be like? With Him existing in every thought, every movement, and every action? With Him being the very reason for life itself?

These girls seemed genuinely happy and I was curious to know more. Until now, I'd had no idea what it actually felt like to be happy—truly, genuinely, and consistently happy. My happiness had always been linked to someone or something, depending on what was going on around me; happiness had never been linked with myself.

Whatever they had going on, I wanted *in*.

We moved into the Bible study portion of the evening. As I sat next to my new friends, we began reading from Luke 9. The reading, observations, and applications of our group discussion spoke right to my heart, answering questions I had been sitting on all week. We discussed how Jesus spoke of love, truth, and honour, serving others and bringing both physical and metaphorical healing to many. I had been struggling to work through these concepts.

During a conversation with Brandon earlier that week, we had discussed the topic of how Christians were known for what they were against, as opposed to what they were for. When this subject came up in the study, I felt confident contributing my two cents.

I knew only of what Christianity stood against. I felt that Christians spewed a lot of hate and crazy out into the world. Crazies picketed outside Planned Parenthood clinics, radicals set up shop in the malls, or went door to door pushing their opinions on others. It was only now that I began to realize that the opposite was actually true, that the love, joy, and peace preached by the gospel is what Jesus was *for*. What the church stands for became so clear to me in that moment. God was answering my questions through these new friends. I was ecstatic.

> Whatever they had going on, I wanted *in*.

I find it unfortunate that, in today's times, this is the general view of people who call themselves Christian. There are radical people in any religion who morph and manipulate the teachings to mean what they want and act out accordingly. It is not in Jesus's teaching to shame those who aren't like you, to shame the decisions of people in the secular world, or to make people feel bad. Jesus teaches *love*.

Yet I have learned that it's always easier to avoid looking inward to see that the same hate we feel for other religions also exists in our own. *That* is what's wrong. It's the problem with all religions. It's no one's place to pass judgment.

I felt a new confidence and sense of safety that night. I realized how easy it was to contribute to a conversation about the Bible, even though I was still a beginner. I grabbed the phone numbers of these new friends and went home with overflowing excitement, a high. I had never made friends that easily or found the words within myself to participate in conversations with new people so effortlessly. My new-found confidence banished every worry and fear I had of confusion or not being accepted. I knew I had stumbled upon something good.

On Sunday I met up with my new friends at church, and they introduced me to all their friends, and we all sat together near the front row. I was excited to be there. I had even jumped out of bed that morning looking forward to the unknown of what would happen next, without any fear or anxiety.

There are many passages of the New Testament that played a part in the revelations and decisions I made during this period. Hebrews 11 was a notable one:

Now faith is confidence in what we hope for and assurance about what we do not see. This is what the ancients were commended for.

By faith we understand that the universe was formed at God's command, so that what is seen was not made out of what was visible...

And without faith it is impossible to please God, because anyone who comes to him must believe that he exists and that he rewards those who earnestly seek him.

By faith Noah, when warned about things not yet seen, in holy fear built an ark to save his family. By his faith he condemned the world and became heir of the righteousness that is in keeping with faith.

By faith Abraham, when called to go to a place he would later receive as his inheritance, obeyed and went, even though he did not know where he was going. By faith he made his home in the promised land like a stranger in a foreign country; he lived in tents, as did Isaac and Jacob, who were heirs with him of the same promise... And by faith even Sarah, who was past childbearing age, was enabled to bear children because she considered him faithful who had made the promise...

All these people were still living by faith when they died. They did not receive the things promised; they only saw them and welcomed them from a distance, admitting that they were foreigners and strangers on earth. People who say such things show that they are looking for a country of their own. If they had been thinking of the country they had left, they would have had opportunity to return. Instead, they were longing for a better country—a heavenly one. Therefore God is not ashamed to be called their God, for he has prepared a city for them.

By faith Abraham, when God tested him, offered Isaac as a sacrifice. He who had embraced the promises was about to sacrifice his one and only son...

By faith Moses, when he had grown up, refused to be known as the son of Pharaoh's daughter. He chose to be mistreated along with the people of God rather than to enjoy the fleeting pleasures of sin. He regarded disgrace for the sake of Christ as of greater value than the treasures of Egypt, because he was looking ahead to his reward...

These were all commended for their faith, yet none of them received what had been promised, since God had planned something better for us so that only together with us would they be made perfect.

—Hebrews 11:1–3, 6–9,
11, 13–17, 24–26, 39–40

As I read these words, I subconsciously nodded along, feeling empowered with each statement of faith. Then it dawned on me that in all my life I had never questioned these fundamental stories, never questioned a burning talking bush, or God splitting the sea so the people of Israel could walk through. I never questioned the prophets being able to hear the literal voice of God, or God commanding someone to build a boat and gather dangerous animals who somehow didn't harm each other so that He could wipe out the entire population and start fresh.

If we truly take a look at these testimonies of faith with our logic caps on, we realize that they seem absolutely ridiculous.

If I never questioned any of these growing up—since I knew these tales to be true—then why was I questioning everything written about Jesus? The story of Jesus suddenly felt equally as plausible, or ridiculous, as these fundamental Judaic teachings. Was it not possible that the story of Jesus was the continuation of those stories and teachings?

This revelation felt like a weight off my shoulders. I may have opened my heart, but it wasn't until this moment that God lifted the veil that had been covering my eyes.

The next few weeks flew by. Every verse I read and every book I whizzed through spoke volumes. Every conversation, every question I asked, left me in awe of my new ability to understand the Bible. It all started to make sense, like a series of puzzle pieces fitting together to form a larger picture. God was showing me the pieces I had been missing out on all along. He was beginning to complete *my* puzzle.

What was still missing though, was my Aha! moment—the concrete feeling I needed in order to say that I believed in this Jesus fellow of the Bible. I needed a close encounter. I still had moments of doubt, only now I knew that God was real and working His way through all the kinks in my life, slowly cracking away at the hard walls I had forced up.

But Jesus? I still wasn't a hundred percent sure. I needed more.

My
Saving Grace

Chapter Seven

I wished that every day was Sunday. It was my favourite day of the week and never came fast enough. My new sense of calm had replaced my anxiety, my heart growing fuller as I settled into my new routine.

But one particular Sunday was special. I walked up to my new friends and sat down for the service, like always. The service ran as usual and the band returned to the stage to sing a song at the end, a song I had never heard before. The moment they began to play, I was mesmerized, consumed by the peaceful melody and relatable lyrics.

The song stirred up something strange within. Chills rushed through me and goosebumps broke out from head to toe. I was in a trance. It felt like I was standing in an empty room, just me and God. Peace overwhelmed me as the lyrics spoke to my soul. The peace, love, and acceptance of Jesus finally weaved their way inside me and became one with my heart.

There are hardly any words strong enough to do justice to what I experienced that day. All I know is that everything up until that point in my life was finished and I stepped into the next chapter of my life. It was like a flash-forward in a movie, when you get to see the characters twenty or thirty years down the road living the happy ending they were always meant to live. I could finally see my future and feel Jesus. For the first time in my life, I knew where I was heading.

As I stood there, surrounded by my new friends, receiving these powerful words as if God was speaking them directly into my heart, I knew. What I had come across was the answer to what I had always searched for. My heart was full. All the scattered puzzle pieces of my life, old and new, instantaneously fit together into one whole and perfect picture. Jesus was real, He was wonderful, and there was no doubt in my mind that I would choose to leave everything behind to follow Him.

I encountered the Holy Spirit that day, and He filled every empty, depressed, and anxiety-ridden hole I had spent my entire life battling against. In one moment, I was free. God spoke to me through song, reassuring me that I was safe now, that I was His. I knew in my heart that I was right where I was meant to be.

> This happiness was dependent on nothing other than myself and Jesus. I was now complete.

April 23, 2018 was the day I accepted Jesus into my life and made my everlasting commitment to follow Him. What I felt was true and genuine happiness, the happiness I had seen in my new friends, the happiness I had always wanted. This happiness was dependent on nothing other than myself and Jesus. I was now complete.

From Death to Life

Chapter Eight

What Chase had been asking me to do for him—to change my life, change my views, and walk away from my family—was too much. I would not and could not do that. I was too strong-willed and proud of my heritage to change just for someone else to accept me. And rightly so.

However, when Jesus became an answer for *me*, *my* saving grace, *my* personal Saviour, nothing could compare. My head was clear for the first time in my life and I knew where I was going.

It wasn't long before Jesus became the drive and passion behind every word I spoke and action I took, just as I had observed in my new friends the day I met them. I had spent twenty-four years being lost and finally found my way home to where I truly belonged.

A passage in Matthew 4 illustrates the calling of the first disciples. Jesus came across Peter and Andrew fishing beside the sea and called to them:

> *"Come, follow me," Jesus said, "and I will send you out to fish for people." At once they left their nets and followed him.*

—Matthew 4:19–20

The nets in this story represent our ties, chains, or struggles of the world, and when Peter and Andrew left their nets behind to follow Jesus, they symbolically left behind their worries, fears, and ties to the world to follow Jesus.

Nothing but Jesus matters. He is the defender, protector, comforter, and answer to all. All I needed to finally find my freedom was to understand that and give my trust and worries to Him. At this point, it was a no-brainer. I wanted to toss my nets behind and walk freely into the arms of my Lord and Saviour who had always been standing right beside me, patiently waiting for me to find Him.

My identity had always been in Christ, I just hadn't known it.

I remember the next visit back to my therapist so clearly. I sat in her office, nervous to share my new findings, seeing as every other session had been full of my disbelief. I sat down and shared with her that I now believed in everything I had previously rejected. The look on her face was as if she had seen a ghost. She pulled out a questionnaire for me to answer, which I think of as the "Is Simone crazy?" questionnaire.

> My identity had always been in Christ, I just hadn't known it.

This session opened my eyes to the solidity of my beliefs. My therapist gave me feedback and advice, just like she always had, but this time it felt meaningless. There was no Jesus in her perspective. Her advice wasn't rooted in the same background as the Bible. As I sat there thinking about what Jesus would want from me, I realized this would be my last session with her. From now on, I would seek out Christian counselling, which I highly recommend to any and everyone. Counselling isn't just for people with serious problems; it's a healthy outlet for everyday people looking to healthily think through what's going on in their lives.

It was only a matter of time before Chase came back into the picture. I was lying in bed one evening, talking to God and praying that He'd make everything work out with Chase. It had been weeks since Chase and I had last spoke directly, although I had shamefully been sending him messages about what I had been experiencing, which he would open but never reply to.

But this night, I picked up my phone and there he was. I cried, thinking, *Wow, God, is this how the prayer thing works?*

I quickly replied to him, sharing all my exciting news. But to my surprise, he didn't hesitate to burst my bubble. He accused me of lying and manipulating him.

Excuse me? If I was going to lie, would I not have done that months ago? Who would do something like that? His scepticism cut so deeply. His lack of trust and kindness towards me was difficult for me to process.

But as time passed and we spoke more, his hesitations seemed to subside.

We spent hours talking about everything new I was learning. My excitement was high and my desire to learn and grow was even higher. I spent all my free time reading my Bible or other related books, finding my groove with prayer and hanging out with my new friends talking about all of the above.

However, my need for perfectionism was also at an all-time high. My need to know everything right away, to have every answer, made all my new activities easy. This was neither good nor bad.

Seeking after Jesus was only positive, but I was unsure of my motives to be doing *so* much. Was it because I needed to know everything in order to feel worthy, or was it my desire to know and love Jesus more intimately? Regardless, I was excited.

The one thing that dampened my excitement a bit was all the lying and sneaking around I had to do when it came to my family. All I wanted to do was shout about Jesus from the rooftops, but instead I hid my Bible underneath a pile of papers in my drawer, or under my pillow, afraid of the war I knew was coming. The pressure of keeping this secret made me uncomfortable, but I was determined to spare my parents the pain for as long as possible.

Inevitably, the truth did surface. First to my mom, who I had been spending more quality time with, as my dad had been throwing himself into his work ever since their separation announcement. She noticed the changes in me and asked about where I had been going now that I'd finished with university; I had been going out more than usual.

"I'm going to church," I finally blurted, as if the words held no weight.

She seemed unable to comprehend the four words that had just fallen from my mouth. We sat in silence for a moment before she began to cry, asking more questions through her tears. I answered them with an excited smile on my face, unable to adjust myself to the emotional distress I had just caused her.

Once the questions were answered and the emotions settled, I left the house and continued on with my night with less weight on my own shoulders. Outside of me making more honest comments around her, we didn't speak of this again for months. Communication had never been a strength in our household.

⌁

In late May 2018, I took a big step in my relationship with Chase. I flew to Calgary to spend time in his world and meet his family. I was about to meet the people who had been so against our relationship from the moment they found out about it. I was nervous, because the picture Chase had been painting for me over the last year wasn't pretty. He was afraid of his parents, and so was I. I was about to walk into the lion's den to try and prove myself to the people who had already made their minds up about me. To them, I was never good enough, which played into my insecurities and caused me to desperately seek their approval and love all the more.

The first morning after I arrived, I sat at Chase's kitchen table with my Bible, waiting for him to get home from class. It wasn't long before his father came down the stairs and struck up a conversation with me, first about myself and then about Chase. The dynamic of their relationship became obvious to me from the way his father spoke. Where I had been trying to push Chase to gain control of his own life, I could see that there was only one real man in this house, and he made all the decisions.

The interaction made me uncomfortable. However, it was interesting to have a firsthand view of what Chase had been trying to tell me all along.

Chase's mom came down next. She sat and we engaged in a lengthy conversation, mostly about myself and the journey I was on, mixed with a few readings from the Bible. I stared at her in awe as I began to realize the burning passion this woman had for the Lord—and she wasn't afraid to show it. I felt sad knowing that this passion hadn't seemed to rub off on Chase, but I was convinced that we would one day get there together.

I could see myself having conversations around that table, just like this one, for the rest of my life.

It was interesting to see the dynamic between Chase and his father versus the one between his parents. In contrast to my original encounter with Chase's dad just minutes earlier, his parents weren't as scary as I had imagined. They loved Jesus and they loved each other, which I found admirable. The tiny glimpse into their relationship I was able to see—the way they spoke, encountered each other, and spent time with God together—gave me a real and concrete idea of what a godly relationship should look like.

Chase got home shortly after and we spent the day exploring the city. It was obvious to him that his family no longer disapproved of me, so he began to relax. We discussed mending our relationship, and from there the rest of my trip was history. Things escalated quickly and soon we were planning for when we'd get a dog, have kids, get married, etc. My heart raced with each comment, finally seeing everything fall into place.

Thank You, Jesus, for answering my prayers and giving me everything I had been dreaming of, I prayed.

We left off on a good note and I flew back home, but it was only a matter of time before our toxic cycle took a new course. Chase soon retracted everything he had said on the trip, ripping my heart out of my chest and hanging me out to dry yet again. I couldn't understand why we always ended up taking ten steps back every time it seemed like we were moving forward. I knew in my heart that Chase couldn't have planned for marriage, kids, and a future and spent the better half of my trip with his mouth glued to mine if he didn't really want that, right? He was just scared, right?

Time went on and we carried on as always. Even when we were broken up, we still remained in consistent contact, discussing our future as normal. It made no sense and constantly confused me.

Chase returned to Winnipeg with his family that July, but prior to their arrival he made it clear that we would not be spending any time together. Of course that was not the case and we spent every day of his two-week trip together, laughing, joking, planning, and "kissing" as normal.

The topic of our conversations suddenly changed to, "Which one of us is moving?" But we were at a stalemate on that. Chase wasn't keen on returning to Winnipeg, and I hesitated at the thought of moving to Calgary. I had a good job with full-time hours and a free place to live; it was too inconvenient for me, the one swimming in debt, to pick up and leave, whereas Chase was unemployed and had only been saving throughout his year off.

Soon after my return from Calgary, my dad clued in to where my life had been going. On our way to the car after a family dinner, he wrapped his arm around me and said, "Now, don't go doing anything crazy like converting and believing all that crap." He was fishing, and seeking reassurance that I was still his sweet little Jewish baby.

71

"What if I already have?" I replied, shifting the dynamic of our relationship.

The drive home was very quiet, my sister poking fun at the situation, driving the angry roots deeper and deeper until he finally exploded. It felt as though he was ashamed of my decisions, shaking his hands in the air and yelling about his views on Christians. Nothing I said in reply mattered because I had been "naive and brainwashed by those crazy people." Apparently I didn't know what I was talking about. He had taken one course in university where they read parts of the Bible, which suddenly made him an expert on the subject while the months of studying, learning, and encountering I'd been experiencing made me naive and stupid? I felt my heart sink into my stomach. I'd known this wasn't going to be an easy conversation, but something about this rejection pierced me in a new way.

To a Jewish parent, one of the worst things that can happen is for a child to leave the faith. This was clear from the fact that my dad could barely say a word or look me in the eye for months. That night changed everything.

Contrary to what most people believe, nobody has "left" or "run" from Judaism. The Torah and the rest of what has been labelled "Old Testament" is the glue that binds Jesus and His teachings together; altogether they both form the Bible. I haven't run away from HaShem;[8] I'm running right towards Him, the Author, Creator, and Father of it all. There will never come a day when I am

---

8   HaShem is one of the many Hebrew terms for God. It literally translates to "The Name."

no longer Jewish. I am and will always be a Jew. I am only a *completed* Jew now; my heritage and faith in Jesus go hand in hand.

There's a common misconception that the New Testament is yet another book on how to persecute the Jews, but what many are too scared to read into and see revealed is that Jesus didn't come for the Gentiles or to turn people away from their Judaic roots. He came *for* the Jews, as the solution *for* Israel's hardships. He is the Jewish Messiah!

Over time, the identity of Jesus has been lost in translation. He is a born Jew, prophesied to be the Saviour of the Jews, who will in fact bring the entire world together in one faith. This is the truest, purest form of God's prophecy to Abraham in Genesis 17:

> *When Abram was ninety-nine years old, the Lord appeared to him and said, "I am God Almighty; walk before me faithfully and be blameless. Then I will make my covenant between me and you and will greatly increase your numbers."*
>
> *Abram fell facedown, and God said to him, "As for me, this is my covenant with you: You will be the father of many nations."*
>
> —Genesis 17:1–4

God spoke over Abraham that he would become the father over many nations, not just one nation (the Jews). Through Jesus, Abraham has become the father of *all* nations! From Abraham came David, and from David came Jesus. The New Testament is written by Jews for Jews.

What is there to fear? Why are we afraid of faith? Is that not what God has been asking from us all along? If we as Jews believe so strongly in the Torah and the commandments God has given, why does someone like Jesus pose a threat? Secure people do not create waves as big as that of the testimonies of the Pharisees in the New Testament. Is it because Jesus doesn't fit the bill of the ideologies of what the Messiah was assumed to be? Are we afraid because it might be true? These are the actual words prophesied in Isaiah 53:

Who has believed our message and to whom has the arm of the Lord been revealed? He grew up before him like a tender shoot, and like a root out of dry ground. He had no beauty or majesty to attract us to him, nothing in his appearance that we should desire him. He was despised and rejected by mankind, a man of suffering, and familiar with pain. Like one from whom people hide their faces he was despised, and we held him in low esteem.

Surely he took up our pain and bore our suffering, yet we considered him punished by God, stricken by him, and afflicted. But he was pierced for our transgressions, he was crushed for our iniquities; the punishment that brought us peace was on him, and by his wounds we are healed. We all, like sheep, have gone astray, each of us has turned to our own way; and the Lord has laid on him the iniquity of us all.

He was oppressed and afflicted, yet he did not open his mouth; he was led like a lamb to the slaughter, and as a sheep before its shearers is silent, so he did not open his mouth. By oppression and judgment he was taken away. Yet who of his generation protested? For he was cut off from the land of the living; for the transgression of my people he was punished. He was assigned a grave with the wicked, and with the rich in his death, though he had done no violence, nor was any deceit in his mouth.

Yet it was the Lord's will to crush him and cause him to suffer, and though the Lord makes his life an offering for sin, he will see his offspring and prolong his days, and the will of the Lord will prosper in his hand. After he has suffered, he will see the light of life and be satisfied; by his knowledge my righteous servant will justify many, and he will bear their iniquities. Therefore I will give him a portion among the great, and he will divide the spoils with the strong, because he poured out his life unto death, and was numbered with the transgressors. For he bore the sin of many, and made intercession for the transgressors.

—Isaiah 53:1–12

Jesus is the promise spoken above, precisely: a Messiah not to appear as we might think or desire, a Messiah who will be rejected by mankind, a Messiah not just to bring peace but to also suffer and die for us... to die by being pierced for our transgressions, and by His wounds we are healed! He is a Messiah who was led like a lamb to the slaughter but didn't open His mouth upon all these afflictions. He was assigned a grave even though He was innocent, and in His moments upon death He finds satisfaction in knowing that it is finished, because this was God's will for our coming Messiah.

Jesus preached change. He preached something different than what the Torah was saying, and at the end of the day people don't like change. The Rabbis of the time thought He was a sacrilegious blasphemer, but I would argue that they never took a second to ask the Lord who this man really was. The topic remained untouched because of their fear of the unknown.

Isaiah's prophecy is undeniably the story hiding inside the New Testament. The most powerful truth of the Jewish people is laid out right here, yet it's discredited daily and chalked up to an "interpretation" by Christians who are only trying to convert the Jews. To deny what this prophecy actually says is to deny what the purpose of the Torah is in its entirety. To deny this is an admission that they don't, in fact, trust our God and all He spoke to and through. The facts are laid out as clear as day; it is now upon us to open our eyes, open our hearts, and accept it.

What if, just for a second, every Jew or Gentile let their guards down and read through the Torah and the Gospels through the eyes of openness and a willingness to understand the other?

Weeks later, as Chase and I continued to struggle and discuss the next steps of our relationship, there was a shift in management at my work. A lot changed in a short period of time and I found out there wouldn't be enough hours for me to work full-time anymore, let alone even three days a week. I couldn't believe that this job, which had offered me security for four years and promised me indefinite full-time hours, was about to end, leaving me without a steady source of income.

The job that was tying me to Winnipeg no longer existed. I was afraid but felt that it meant it was time for me to move forward with my life.

Not long after that, an argument went awry with my parents and my dad asked me to leave. I returned home after a late shift, grabbed some pizza, and sat down to eat my 10:00 p.m. dinner. An argument about my faith sparked, resulting in my dad standing over me, shaking his fists, and screaming: "If this is the life you want to live, you can't do it under this roof. I'm sure one of your new 'friends' will happily take you in!"

I don't have many memories of rage and violence coming from my dad. In fact, it's less than a handful, because my dad is generally a man of peace. However, this was a fearful moment for me. As I sat with my pizza in my lap, shaking and afraid, I made some defensively snide remark, ran up to my room, and packed my bags in hysterics. Angry that I hadn't even taken two bites of my pizza, I sat on the edge of my bed and sent out a few messages in search of somewhere to go, rocking myself back and forth, repeating "I can do all things through Christ who strengthens me, I can do all things through Christ who strengthens me…" By now the tears had made their way down my chest and were soaking my legs.

With my bags packed, I rushed downstairs and out the door, yelling "Jesus loves you" on my way out. I slammed the door behind me, strong enough that I shook the entire house.

I had argued with Chase for him to move back to Winnipeg because of my stable job and home security, but now neither existed. I had to seriously consider moving and imagine a life in Calgary. The idea still seemed a bit too far off to be real—that is, until I met a new friend at church who happened to have a room available in her home… in Calgary. This new development had me believing that all signs pointed to God calling me out of Winnipeg.

Over the following weeks, it became even more clear that this was, in fact, what God wanted me to do. The safety nets that were holding me back, tying me down to Winnipeg, had been ripped right out from under me. A bright red carpet was rolled out in Calgary's direction.

Again, much like the disciples and their fishing nets, my decision was clear. I called Chase to update him on the situation. He was sceptical of the signs but admitted he would like it if I moved and that it would be nice to have me around more consistently.

It took me one week to find a job, and that was it—the decision was final. I was moving to Calgary.

The Old Has Gone

Ever since that day back in April when I accepted Jesus into my life, I had been mulling over the right time to be baptized. I prayed about it for weeks but kept coming up short. I knew it was going to happen, that it was just a matter of when.

My church had baptisms three weeks in a row, which was unusual, and each week I felt the Holy Spirit urge me more deeply to stand up and publicly declare my faith. I knew God was nudging me, so I made my decision.

On May 26, 2018, I spoke to someone at the church who helped me get set up with a mentor to begin my pre-baptism process. I met weekly with my mentor to go over a series of prescribed topics. During these sessions, I further developed my ability to articulate what I had been feeling and talk about Jesus.

These meetings were like unintentional therapy. The bond we created through safety and trust made it easy to be open and honest about my thoughts and feelings.

Mentors were chosen by the church, and they were people who upheld strong and unwavering faith and had solid moral boundaries. My mentor had an insight into life that was truly Spirit-led and blissful. A lot of our conversations helped mould the foundation of my growing faith. This was a crucial step which instilled a lot of confidence in me.

My baptism date finally arrived on September 2. I arrived early to church to do a walkthrough on stage. I felt myself nearly bursting at the seams. This was my big day!

My friends arrived early and we all went upstairs into the back room for the pre-service prayer. Everyone surrounded me, either with hands up or on me, blessing me for my choice that day and many days to come.

When the service began, I walked up on stage to tell my story in front of the packed audience. My hands were shaking as I nervously spoke about how I had come to accept Jesus into my life, and how He had changed everything.

> I was ready for whatever was coming next!

As I stepped into the baptism tank, the worship team began to play Chris Tomlin's "White Flag," upon my request. My mentor asked me three questions to confirm the choices I had already made, then tilted me back and dunked me underwater. As I came back up, I was immediately overwhelmed with the same feeling of calming peace I had felt back in April.

> *...for all of you who were baptized into Christ have clothed yourselves with Christ.*
>
> —Galatians 3:27

I raised my white flag and surrendered it all to Him. The war was over, the darkness was gone, and the light in my life was bright and new. I washed away my past and clothed myself with Jesus. I was ready for whatever was coming next!

⁓

When I arrived in Calgary on September 10, I ran up to my new house and knocked on the door. Everything felt like it was aligning. Life was great.

I unpacked and settled into my new home, began my new job, and went about my new life. I explored a couple of churches before making a decision; it took me two months before I really felt like calling one my home.

Every Sunday, I eagerly jumped out of bed to worship and praise in my new church community. The song choices were flashy and fun and the pastor preached a deep and raw message. But at the end of each service I ran out as fast as possible; I was always too nervous to be caught standing awkwardly with no one to talk to. The frightening task of making new friends, as an adult, couldn't have been more daunting... or mortifying. No thank you!

Each week I tested the waters, staying five minutes longer than the last, until I eventually worked up the courage to talk to someone. I still maintained regular contact with my friends back in Winnipeg, but I had no appropriate counsel here in Calgary.

Community is important for many reasons. The importance of friendship within your active church community and surroundings is vital in the way you walk with God. The Bible practically shouts at us about the importance Jesus places on surrounding yourself with other believers: *"For where two or three gather in my name, there am I with them"* (Matthew 18:20). Among many other verses, this one states the sole reason that I believe a solid faith community is crucial. Where two or more gather, God is with us, meaning that it's a lot easier for the enemy to attack us when we're alone—alone with our thoughts, alone with our temptations, and alone in our decision-making. It's a lot easier to remain within a trial and temptation, to continue on a wrong path or remain at a spiritual standstill, when we're isolated.

In the area of community, however, I was severely lacking. The anxiety and nerves I felt week in and week out over simply saying "Hello" wasn't the will of God. He asks us to remain in community to spread His love, peace, and kindness out to the world, to build each other up, fight spiritual or mental battles, and call each other to greatness. But it took me nearly six months to make any real friends.

In October, Chase spent the week cat-sitting for a family friend. This presented an opportunity for us to finally spend the night together without fear that his parents would get angry. During this week I picked him up from work and we had dinner, then hung out in bed like we used to. These times with him were my favourite; we were always able to connect differently in this more intimate setting.

On one of those nights, I lay in bed and read my Bible while Chase played video games in the other room. When he wrapped up, he lay down next to me and I asked if I could share with him what I was reading. He agreed, so I began to read.

At the end of the chapter, which was from Matthew, I asked him what he thought.

"I wasn't listening," he said.

I rolled my eyes and told him I would read it to him again.

"No, I've read the Bible before. I don't need to read it again"

Sorry, what? My heart sank. These were the words from the mouth of the guy who had wanted nothing more than for me to be a Christian so we could be together? And yet he *never* wanted to talk about Jesus.

This was devastating for me. The more I explored and matured in my faith, the more eager and excited I was to share it with my future partner. I had begun to picture our life together, a life in which we would read and discuss the Bible, watch videos, listen to sermons, and read books. But to my disappointment, Chase never wanted to bring God into our relationship, or into his life at all.

This began a series of events that led to our demise. I knew in my heart that God wouldn't give me a man who was this unenthusiastic and uninterested in Him, who wouldn't want to share in my journey. Slowly, my heart began to change and my backbone began to strengthen.

Our last day together was a Sunday. I had finally convinced him to join me at my new church, so I picked him up and we sat in the 9:00 a.m. service. Afterward we planned to drive to Lake Louise. It was all fun and games until we arrived in Canmore, about halfway. We went for lunch at a little bagel shop. That's when the mood changed. We began to fight over something so insignificant and small: Instagram.

Chase began to get mean. He didn't want to hear anything I said, didn't want to resolve whatever dumb issue had arisen; he only wanted to tear into me. Any anger that had been festering inside finally flew out of us both. We stormed out of the bagel shop and back into my car for the last hour of the drive, of which I spent its entirety yelling at him.

In hindsight, we should have driven right home, but nonetheless we finally got to Lake Louise where I told Chase I needed a minute before getting out of the car. He demanded that I get out of the car, but I insisted that I needed a minute to calm myself down.

Chase stormed out of the car and began to walk away. I sat in the car crying for nearly thirty minutes. Chase had walked so far away that I had no idea where he went, which made me increasingly anxious and angry.

I decided I was going to wait five more minutes before leaving him behind. Lucky for Chase, he was already on his way back to the car. Through my tears I asked where he had gone.

"I went to the lake. Do you want to see my pictures?" He taunted me with a smirk.

It only took half a second before Chase realized that was the wrong response.

I lost it, yelling louder than I ever had in my entire life: "Get the f— out of my car! I'm leaving you here!"

He thought I was joking.

"I'm not joking! I don't give a sh— about you. Get the f— out!"

"No," he said, laughing. "I have work tomorrow. You're not leaving me here."

This went on for a few minutes. I could tell he was beginning to get afraid, so I grabbed his backpack and began rolling down my window to toss it out. I was livid.

Chase frantically snatched the bag from my hands, apologizing profusely for whatever he thought I was upset about. He truly had no clue; I was done with his crap.

Our drive home was the most serious and tense car ride of my life. We discussed why he'd needed to wait until I had been pushed far beyond my breaking point to admit any fault and take responsibility. Why did it have to get this far for us to have any sort of breakthrough? He opened up, explaining that he felt as though he could only respond to fear, which explained why he submitted so quickly to his father.

This conversation was productive, almost like the light at the end of our very dark relationship tunnel. I was hopeful that this fight would finally get through to him, that maybe he would change, even if it wouldn't be for me.

I dropped Chase off just in time to check out the evening service at my church, which happened to be held inside a nightclub as the usual movie theatre was unavailable; I craved the opportunity to connect with God after such an intensely emotional day.

As the pastor preached in the middle of the club, I knew. I knew that this was the end. He preached from Proverbs 4:23: *"Above all else, guard your heart, for everything you do flows from it."*

These words cut deeply into me. I hadn't ever protected myself when it came to relationships. I had let man after man consume me and control me, causing a continuous broken heart.

No more. It was time to change. It was time to guard my heart, protect myself, and finally stand up for the respect I deserved.

Chase called me later that evening to apologize again, only this time the apology extended further than I could have ever imagined.

He revealed the many lies he had been keeping from me since the first week we'd met. He confessed betrayals and methods by which he had guilted and manipulated me all along.

This phone call was surreal. I barely said anything—shockingly, since I always have something to say. I couldn't believe my ears.

If there was ever a final confirmation from God, this was it.

Our relationship ended that night. Few tears were shed, for I knew in my heart that the Lord would never create a destiny for me involving this much betrayal, heartbreak, and emotional abuse. There was someone else out there, someone designed specifically for me, someone who would build me up and encourage and support me no matter what. Someone who would share my passion for Him, among many other common interests. Someone who was ambitious to pursue His calling effortlessly and help me learn and grow in my faith.

That's the dream I had been too blind to realize could never happen with Chase.

The scary thought was that I needed to submit complete control to God, trusting that in due time I would meet this supposed person.

Somehow that turned out to be the most thrilling and illuminating thought in the darkness that now surrounded me.

The New Is Here

Chapter Ten

This time, something felt different. My heart was broken, as usual, but I felt an overall sense of peace. It was over, it was finally *over*. The Lord was shouting that Chase wasn't the one for me and it was time for me to listen. The man He had designed for me would never cheat, lie, or manipulate me the way Chase had.

Regardless of the good in Chase, there had also been so much bad. Over time the darkness in him had overcome the light, and now it was time to move forward. I prayed day in and day out for God to bring me peace over the breakup during this time of healing...

Until suddenly one day I woke up and it was all okay.

This was the easiest breakup I had ever been through. A typical breakup for me would consist of endless bedridden days full of tears and depression and the loss of understanding that life would continue even without that person. I would indulge in overconsumption of the topic, talking about it to any and everyone who would listen. I would attach myself to and rely on men for my happiness.

Not this time. I had my Lord and Saviour by my side and felt ready to brave any battle the enemy threw my way. I put on my armour and walked through each day with a smile on my face, determined to be prepared for whatever the future held.

Who had I become?

My journey through singleness began with the proclamation that I would be a strong, independent woman who was finally going to find her identity in Christ, unattached from anyone else. This was my time to shine.

I spent hours and days reading book after book about personal development through Christ, biblical history, and how proper Christ-centred relationships should look. I spent hours considering and praying about the kind of man I wanted God to bring into my life, making many decisions with Him.

Self-love is a big theme in my life, and it still is to this day. This term can mean different things to different people. It can be as simple as taking a day off to show yourself love through pampering, napping, etc., or it can go as far as growing deep roots in your value for yourself, so much that you know what you deserve and stand your ground as you wait for it to arrive.

My breakup with Chase led me toward the latter. Our final goodbye was the first time in my life that I walked away from someone with no emotional baggage, the first time I was able to stake my claim on knowing I deserved better. This revelation was life-giving and beautiful, and it showed me how much Jesus really had changed me.

Though my self-love has wavered over time, it is always an important lesson to circle back to.

You might ask how it's possible to know whether you love yourself. For me, it was the realization that Chase and I just didn't work, that the constant bickering and fighting wasn't healthy. No matter how many times he came back, he never apologized or was able to admit fault in any of his actions.

Self-love is knowing what you deserve and loving yourself enough to not allow toxicity into your bubble. It's knowing that God created you in His perfect image and loves you unconditionally. How do we know that? Because He loves us so much that He sent his only Son to this earth to live and die for us as the ultimate sacrificial gift (John 3:16). That is true love. You have to know that God loves you, so that you're not seeking love, affection, attention, or approval from any other human, romantic or otherwise.

Your approval is in God, your love is in God, and your attention is towards only God. That is self-love. That's where everything else flows from. Our ability to love and show kindness to others flows directly from the way we love ourselves.

> "Teacher, which is the greatest commandment in the Law?"
>
> Jesus replied: "'Love the Lord your God with all your heart and with all your soul and with all your mind.' This is the first and greatest commandment. And the second is like it: 'Love your neighbor as yourself.' All the Law and the Prophets hang on these two commandments."

> —Matthew 22:36–40

See, first you must love God and then you must love your neighbour *as* yourself. This is normally read as the "love thy neighbour" verse and we skim over the important prerequisite hiding inside this great commandment: we must love our neighbours *as* ourselves! How can we love our neighbours if we first do not love ourselves? God's greatest commandment to us is to love *ourselves*. To ignore this is to ignore a direct commandment from our God.

When I first met Jesus, I had a lot of value for myself and I was on fire; no one could touch me. As time went on, the more often I had to remind myself of this love. It also became easier to get lost in my old ways. We must actively find ways to love ourselves and put this principle into practice, even if it means removing someone from our lives and hurting them as collateral. First we must love God, then we must love ourselves (not to be confused with selfishness), and finally we are to love others.

The Bible is full of important life lessons that are still relevant two thousand years after it was written. How powerful is that? When I found out that the Bible has been the number one best-selling book year after year, I was awestruck. It is God's living word. It is supernatural. In its pages there's a lesson for anything you may be going through. You only need to ask God and take a look.

⁓

I finally joined a small group and started making connections. The more I connected, the more I learned about myself and others, but mostly I learned about what my church had to offer. There are a lot of options when it comes to connecting through most churches, but it still comes down to the level of effort you're willing to put in to get yourself out there.

I put in a lot of effort, but I struggled when it came to making friends. I constantly chased after what seemed like the ideal group, but most of my conversations remained shallow with no follow-through when it came down to planning a hangout. I extended many invitations and logged an exceptional number of hours facing strangers across tables, but most never reached out again. I poured my heart and soul into complimenting and trying to please others only to never have a text or thought returned. I'd come home feeling more empty and alone than when I'd begun.

At least I was always able to come home and connect with my roommates. But they had their own lives and I found myself home alone most weekends, wishing I had my own social network. I rested these worries and pains with God, which made it bearable. However, this was a very lonely season for me.

The sad reality is that the friends I chased after, the ones I thought were "perfect," soon revealed themselves to have their own dysfunctional immaturities. They were too exclusive, they gossiped, and they made ill comments about others. At the end of the day, I didn't want to be involved with that. Those were the kinds of relationships I had left behind when I chose to follow Jesus. That sort of behaviour isn't what He has called us to in His church. Those aren't the kind of friends you want, and they aren't the kind of people you grow a deep meaningful community around. Those are the people with whom you amicably smile and wave at across the room while you continue searching for the real keepers. You will find them.

In January 2019, I drove up to Edmonton for a weekend to attend a conference designed to help people grow deeper in their faith. I arrived feeling a bit anxious about spending the weekend alone in a crowd full of thousands of strangers.

Little did I know that experiencing this alone was exactly what God had planned. This weekend shifted the entire trajectory of my faith. It was life-changing.

The first night, a well-known Christian worship group called Jesus Culture got up on stage and began to sing. To my surprise, I knew almost all the songs. Eager to finally participate without my eyes being glued to the screen, I shut my eyes and began to sing along.

Slowly I relaxed, and layer by layer my walls broke down. Suddenly my hands raised up in front of my body, whereas typically I would stand very still, feeling self-conscious with my arms crossed. I began to feel that same overwhelming peace I had back in April, the day I had met Jesus.

This night of worship opened me up to what would become my deepest form of connection with the Lord. He was there at the conference with me, reassuring me that I was still on the right path.

My experience that night was unlike anything I had felt before. I let my inhibitions go and left everything at the feet of Jesus.

Not long after this conference, my half-raised holding-a-baby worship posture evolved into a full-fledged dance-like-nobody's-watching, wave-your-arms-in-the-air, sing-as-passionately-as-your-heart desires posture. That's where the real magic happens, my friends. Nothing compares to the freedom you feel when you let everything go and praise God through movement and songs to worship Him. It is simply transformational.

> I let my inhibitions go and left everything at the feet of Jesus.

The rest of the weekend lived up to the awesomeness of its beginning. Each session taught me something new and relevant to exactly what I was going through. I learnt about blessings and curses, speaking only uplifting and encouraging words into the lives of others, and going back to retract already-spoken curses. I learned about healthy relationships, both romantic and platonic, and in a very quiet moment of prayer and reflection I very clearly heard Him tell me, "Stop trying so hard."

I was initially confused by this, as I had never heard Him manifest as a physical voice before. I thought about it for a while. God was telling me to stop trying so hard, to stop chasing after the superficial relationships that had been destroying me. If I stopped trying so hard, the right people would come. That was mind-blowing! What may seem like common sense to you felt like a new revelation for me.

I had never been in a situation like this where I had no friends. Not even one. I didn't know how to start from zero. My past friendships had usually formed as our paths crossed, so now that I'd picked up my life and moved to a new city, I had assumed I would have to put in a lot of serious effort to socialize.

After the conference, I returned to Calgary just in time to run to church for the evening service. I was on fire, feeling high off the Holy Spirit. This was the first service where I didn't care about anything other than the actual service itself. I stopped trying so hard! Imagine that.

It seems silly to write up this memory, knowing now how ridiculous I was to care for shallow things like getting an in with the right crew, but this was an important lesson for me in trusting the Lord and hearing and acting on His direct words to me.

It wasn't long before everything began to fall into place. I found my spot as I served on the church's tech team, running the multimedia and technical supports. It seemed as though my newfound I-don't-care-anymore attitude radiated brilliantly and attracted an entirely new group of people who actually wanted to get to know me. I found my place, and I felt understood—finally!

~

Some of the small groups offered by my church are structured and others can be designed by the person choosing to lead, whether it be sports, fitness, hangouts, or studies.

One particular series of groups are structured by a church in Alabama to walk you through a twelve-week workbook that helps you unveil and work through past hurts. Through this process, you open yourself up to the freedom and healing of Christ. The course ends with a two-day conference, and that's where the real magic happens.

After much consideration and a series of recommendations, unsure of what I was signing up for, I joined this Freedom group for February 2019. On the first day, I walked up to the house, nervous for who might be inside. When I entered to encounter a room full of fresh faces, I realized this would test every fear I had formed around meeting new people.

As the weeks went on, it became a lot clearer that the members of this group who attended our church's north campus seemed a lot more content with the community aspect than what I had been feeling at my current campus. It didn't take me long to make the switch to attending the north campus services. Already on my first Sunday, I was asked by several people to have coffee. I exchanged numbers and even had a few conversations. It was that easy. I made friends; I made many friends.

I jumped headfirst into the north campus tech team, looking forward to the cozy breakfasts and fun atmosphere that embodied each service's setup process. After breakfast we would head into the gymnasium to get the stage, screens, lights, projectors, and tech table ready at the back of the room. This was my favourite part. We laughed, sang, and danced. I was excited to know we were single-handedly creating the space that would invite so many people to know Jesus.

My weekly Freedom group material became applicable to my weekly struggles as the Lord continued to teach and mould me to become more spiritually mature. The struggles came, as they always did, but they also left as I became better equipped to handle them.

This was a comfortable growth season, making friends and growing deeper in my relationship with God. Who was I becoming? I was slowly stepping into my identity, my identity in Christ, becoming a strong warrior, and finding my strength and security in *Him*. I couldn't ask for anything more. I was living the dream!

There Is Freedom

Chapter Eleven

As the Freedom group's curriculum came to an end, we looked forward to the forthcoming conference. A person typically paid for the conference fee along with their workbook before the course began, but I had left this until the last minute because money was tight.

As I drove home from work on the last night before the conference, I realized that I hadn't paid for it yet. I had just enough gas to get there and $10 in my bank account.

I sat on my couch crying, trying to figure out what I was going to do. That's when I received a text message from my group leader letting me know that she had forgotten to tell me that my conference fee had been anonymously covered. She even had a gift waiting for me at the office.

I cried even harder at the way God shows up. He continuously shows up, no matter what. His hands were directly on my situation, and yet again He had made a way.

I wiped my tears and headed down for the first day of the two-day conference. I knew God had something great in store for me that weekend.

Things like this had begun to happen to me often. When they say that God provides, He sure does. There have been countless times during my life in Calgary when envelopes were anonymously left, food dropped off, or lunches covered by friends who knew I was in a tight spot.[9]

Moving to Calgary was quite possibly the worst financial decision I could have made, but I had chosen to trade that struggle in for my happiness. As every month went by, I checked my bank account and seemingly had *just* enough, down to the last cent, to pay my bills. Each month it was a surprise to see how I'd managed to pull that off.

That, my friends, is the work of God.

The best part about it was that I had not a worry in the world. I had the utmost peace because I trusted that I had been brought to Calgary for a reason and that God would resolve my financial burdens eventually.

It is said that peace is not the absence of trouble, but rather the presence of Christ. This has become one of my favourite sayings, and they're words I have come to live by. When I chose to move to Calgary, I chose to follow God's path for me. I chose my happiness and the ability to explore a side of myself that was being weighed down by my family's unhappiness in Winnipeg. It was singlehandedly the best overall decision I ever made, next to my decision to follow Jesus.

---

9   Most of my debt stemmed from university, mixed in with some bad shopping habits I have since learned from.

Let me pause from the story for a few moments and look forward one year. In just that short time, I was happily living my life with a secure and stable job, friends who would drop anything to be there for me, and living in the blissful state of God's presence and calling. I have been stress-free for nearly two full years.

My favourite part? I'm doing my very best to serve and give glory to God in all that I do. That is my only goal as a believer and follower of Jesus Christ. Nothing could be better. Nothing is more rewarding than exemplifying the love, compassion, and patience that Christ shows each and every one of us through our words, actions, and thoughts.[10]

There is so much power in prayer. It is the answer to virtually any problem. Many nights, I lay in bed talking to God about my hopes and dreams and the desires He has given me. The more you pursue Him, the more you become aware of His blessings.

My lack of stress isn't just dumb luck; it's the presence of Christ. It wasn't luck that I found a community that has blessed me financially. Each and every one of the people in my life are blessings from God—and through His divine appointments, they are able to help me in my times of need. We need only ask.

---

10   By no means am I perfect, but I try.

Ask and it will be given to you; seek and you will find; knock and the door will be opened to you.

—Matthew 7:7

But just because we ask doesn't mean we automatically receive. Not everything we want lines up with what God has ordained or what He has planned for us. That may seem difficult to fathom in the moment, but when the true plan unfolds we come to understand.

When we follow the call God places on our lives, when we pursue Him with complete surrender and passion, He gives us the desires of our hearts (Psalm 37:4) and open doors for us. This is the true magic behind having faith in the Lord.

⁓

The Freedom conference is designed to be a Spirit-led experience, emphasizing the value of having a breakthrough over the heart and mind blockages that its participants have dealt with over the previous twelve weeks of small group meetings. The structure of the weekend is a series of sessions each covering a certain topic, followed by someone praying for you and a time of reflection.

As this chapter unfolds, I'll outline the three aspects of the conference that had the most impact on my journey. The power the Holy Spirit had on me during this particular weekend in May 2019 was one very large puzzle piece that fell into place to bring completion to my big picture.

1. Rejection and Forgiveness

Rejection keeps us from investing our lives in others and hinders our relationship with the Lord. Our belief in the words of rejection that have been spoken over us gives the enemy a foot in the door and the ability to manipulate our minds.

We can overcome rejection by believing in God, His truths, and rejecting these lies. The words and actions of others have the power to wound us deeply, but when we hold on to unforgiveness it's like drinking poison and waiting for the other person to die. The other person often doesn't even know how we feel.

Forgiving someone doesn't mean we're saying that their offence was okay, and it doesn't mean that we forget what happened. Rather, it paves the way for a continuous healing process. Forgiveness is an undeserved miracle that only God can place inside of us. It's a choice, not a feeling, that we must choose time and time again. It is, in fact, a requirement:

> *Get rid of all bitterness, rage and anger, brawling and slander, along with every form of malice. Be kind and compassionate to one another, forgiving each other, just as in Christ God forgave you.*
>
> —Ephesians 4:31–32

God forgives us endlessly, so who are we to harbour any of these feelings towards others? Jesus is the perfect example of forgiveness. He has felt everything we feel, experienced everything we experience. He was betrayed by a close friend, falsely accused of many offences, rejected, abused, and humiliated on a cross in front of a crowd. Jesus sees us the way God does, so if we channel that and sharpen our ability to forgive, love and forgiveness will surely follow.

Who came to my mind through this teaching? Who spoke words of rejection over me and left the longest-lasting impression? Both Chase and Lana were obvious candidates in my own life. God had done a lot of the legwork for healing over the last twelve weeks, but on this day I felt the final nudge to break these chains for good.

Anxious butterflies rose in my stomach.

God, I'm not ready to face this, I thought. *Please don't make me!*

But I knew at the bottom of my heart that it was time. I began to think of all the times Lana had neglected me, spoken curses over me and my abilities, and taken advantage of my vulnerability: "You're not good enough. You will never make it. No one will ever want to work with you." These words taunted me, hiding in the back of my mind and slithering out to prevent me from doing anything of real significance. They were always ready to tear me down before I even tried.

I also thought of the times Chase had lashed out in a fight and told me I was paranoid, overreacting, or crazy. I thought about how he had lied to me for two years.

God, I don't want to forgive him...

I knew that I couldn't do it on my own, only through Christ.

As I walked up to my turn for prayer, I chose to start by bringing my feelings about Lana before God. I received my prayer and walked back to my seat to journal through my thoughts. This was the first time I brought my animosity and bitterness towards Lana before Him:

God, thank You for all You have done in my life this last year, all the healing and growth. Thank You for showing me the better way to live by removing my anxiety, depression, insecure thoughts, and actions in the name of Jesus.

I know now is the time to dig deeper and bring forth the next level of healing. You are the almighty God, defender and ruler, conqueror of all. Only You have the power to change my heart.

Please change my heart towards Lana and the pain and abuse she caused me in university, and the long-lasting chains that still exist today. The chains that have been preventing me from pursuing a career in design, or gaining any confidence over what I am capable of. Please help me overcome the curses she spoke over me and guide me in finding my passion for landscape and design all over again. Fill me with Your Spirit and forgive me for believing anything other than your truths that I am good enough, I can make it, and I will succeed in all that you line up for me.

Jesus, only You can show me the way to overcome and only You can break those chains. Amen.

2. Purity

God sees us as pure, regardless of our pasts, because we are new creations in Christ. The Holy Spirit knows when there's something in our lives that keeps us from being fit for God's use, and He will convict us of that sin. Purity is typically associated with sexuality, but it can actually cover our thoughts, our actions, and the words we speak.

We need freedom from ungodly ties. We need cleansing, not condemnation.

What is a soul-tie? It's an attachment to a person who can influence your choices or your will. Soul-ties can be either sexual or emotional.

How do we know when we're involved in an unhealthy emotional soul-tie? You'll do anything to hold on out of a fear of abandonment. You will lie, become dependent, or have boundary and control issues.

How do we denounce these ties and break those chains? By being honest with God and ourselves, repenting of and renouncing them, and engaging in spiritual warfare against the enemy's attacks by reminding ourselves of the truths God speaks over us when we're confronted with a lie.

> We need cleansing,
> not condemnation.

It takes a lot of power to recognize when there is a lie in our midst; identifying that in itself is a skill. We must surrender our minds to Him, repent, cast out the darkness, and pray blessings by speaking His words over ourselves and others daily. If you put on the full armour of God and brave the battle that lies ahead, the enemy *will* flee from you.

Very quickly, the moment I dreaded most had arrived: it was time to let Chase go. I began to shake in my seat, fighting back tears and trying to force myself to be strong.

God, I'm not ready, I thought once again. *I'm not ready to do this. . . please don't make me do this. . .*

We were each given a piece of paper on which to write the names of the ties that needed to be broken. Names of all the men from my past began to flow from my mind onto the paper as I asked God to show me even the ties I may be unaware of. This was a heavy moment as I held the weight of every sexual encounter, feeling, or thought of the last ten years. I poured it all out onto my paper, ending the list off with Chase. It had never occurred to me to write this down before.

As I stood in line for prayer, I felt my anxiety rise and nausea overtake me. I really didn't want to do this. . .

After my turn for prayer, I sat back down, closed my eyes, and began to cry. Then I pulled out my notebook and began to pray:

> God, this is too hard and I do not feel like I am ready to give this up to You, and I do not want to admit that it is over with Chase. I don't want to let this go. It is so much easier to hold on and feel something, and the thought of moving on is so unknown. Please let me keep it.

As I wrote the words, my mind suddenly shifted. I had no idea what came over me, but as I continued to pray, my hand followed:

> Show me that it is time to let go fully. Take my ties to Chase away from me. You know my future, You know the plan, and I trust You. I trust that there is someone better out there for me. Someone You have designed just for

me. Jesus, I renounce these ties and I am ready. Ready to move forward in life and into a new relationship. Ready to lean on You and not my own understanding because only You know what is best for me. Amen.

What had just happened? Those weren't my words, not my thoughts and not my feelings. God was speaking through the words I was writing. I felt the burden of Chase's memory lift off me, and suddenly all the residual pain I had carried from our breakup was *gone*.

God works like that sometimes. He has the power to just remove something from your mind or your heart, taking all your worries and fears and making them disappear. It's divinely supernatural.

3. Fear

Fear can be healthy, like the fear of the Lord and the fear of things that can harm us. Other fears are unhealthy, demonic fears like the fear of losing status, material possessions, relationships, or control.

What was God trying to tell me about my fear? What was I afraid of? As I prayed into this, two thoughts immediately popped into my mind: I was afraid of rejection and afraid of ending up alone or not being good enough.

As I dissected these thoughts during the teaching, my mind raced in remembrance of the times when I had allowed my fear of rejection to take over, causing me to be alone or making me feel abandoned and rejected. Loneliness is my fear's most common symptom and the unfortunate truth is that I allowed myself to be overcome by fears which allowed the enemy in. I clung for dear life to every past relationship from craving the approval of my ashamed and uncommunicative parents to seeking "friends" who were never truly there for me. That's what the enemy wants.

In my moment of clarity and realization, I proclaimed to myself, "Not anymore!"

The opposite of fear is love, and there is no fear in love because perfect love casts out all fear (1 John 4:18). Jesus demonstrated perfect love when He died on the cross for each and every one of us. Perfect love *is* Jesus.

It was time for me to let go—let go of these unhealthy relationships, let go of my fears, and give it up to God who will reign with full power and control over me.

As I stepped up for prayer, I expressed what had come to mind and the woman who was assigned to me placed her hands on my shoulder and began to pray over me. During her prayers, she asked Jesus to allow me to find a verse to counteract every fear or worry the enemy might use to discourage my proclamation. Immediately I heard the words *"fearfully and wonderfully made."*

> *For you created my inmost being; you knit me together in my mother's womb. I praise you because I am fearfully and wonderfully made; your works are wonderful, I know that full well.*
>
> —Psalm 139:13–14

I sat back down in my seat, prayed, and journaled about what I had just experienced:

Jesus, thank You for bringing these fears to mind, and for highlighting the links between not being good enough, being rejected, and being alone. I would never have connected these dots on my own. Break these chains and replace the lies with the truth: I am fearfully and wonderfully made. Your works are wonderful, and I know that full well. God, every time I feel fear, remind me to replace those lies with Your truths.

I will not feel rejected by You or by anyone else. I will not end up alone and I am *more* than enough through You! I will not be overcome by evil, but instead overcome evil with *good*. In Jesus's name, amen.

When these weights lifted off my shoulders, I knew in my heart that everything was going to be okay.

The End

Chapter Twelve

I find that my heart grows fondest of the Bible verses related to seeds, roots, plants, and the environment. They remain the most relatable for me. For a long time, anything related to landscapes had become a sore subject for me after what happened with Lana, but I began to regrow passionate roots in my heart. In its most simplest form, our earth, our environment, and everything built upon it is the deliberate work of God's hands. There is endless beauty in that.

The natural symmetry in nature—in plants, animals, and greater landscapes—is obviously compelling for someone who likes order as much as I do. My favourite and most deeply-seated verse has become John 15:5, so much so that I have since had a symbol of it permanently tattooed on my chest: *"I am the vine; you are the branches. If you remain in me and I in you, you will bear much fruit; apart from me you can do nothing."*

The simplicity of a flowering vine holds such incredible power. Branches that are detached from a vine wither away and die, but the branches that remain attached receive carbon dioxide to release oxygen and nutrients. In other words, without Jesus we have no breath, no fruit, and therefore no life.

My faith in God and in Jesus Christ was the last piece of my big puzzle picture, the final clue that made everything make sense. I needed to understand why I had landed myself in the landscape design stream, why Chase and I had gone through so much hardship, and why I had moved to Calgary.

Creation is one of the wonders of who God is. He spoke our earth into existence, from *nothing*. How amazing is that?

The random tug I had felt to try something new led me to find my passion and path in life—not in the way I thought it would, but in the way that roots me deeper in my faith every single day. The land we walk on, the air we breathe, and everything in between is divinely designed by our Lord Almighty, and as human beings on this earth it is our duty to steward that appropriately, not to take advantage and pollute the earth, but to tend to it and care for it.

This thought never would have occurred to me if it hadn't been for everything that I've illustrated in this book. That's what comes next for me—I want to devote my life to advocating for and achieving care for what God has created environmentally. It never would have occurred to me if I hadn't endured those treacherous three years of my design degree, or met Chase and followed my heart which led me straight to Jesus.

When I look back, I can see how every seemingly random gut feeling, impulsive decision, or unusual thought were the result of God pointing me in the direction my life was meant to lead. These decisions may not have felt significant along the way, but when accumulated I would say they led to something bigger. God is there even when we don't know it, constantly leading us in our best direction. He is our comfort, our rock, and our foundation.

The End

As I end this chapter of my life and walk forward into the next phase of maturing in my faith, it has become clear to me that there are a few key people who have changed the way I will forever view the world.

I wouldn't be where I am today, following God's path, if it weren't for all the good, bad, and boring that brought me here. I am grateful for every experience, conversation, fight, thought, and encounter I've had. I wouldn't trade any of it in for the world.

The Power of Words

I want to reiterate the importance that the power of our thoughts and words have on other people. God created us all equal. He created us in His perfect image and loves each of us the same. And it is our duty to use our words to speak blessings and life into others, to ensure that we build people up wholesomely (Ephesians 4:29) and speak positivity over them, regardless of how we might feel.

> *The tongue has the power of life and death, and those who love it will eat its fruit.*
>
> —Proverbs 18:21

It is said that what goes on in our hearts is represented through our speech. In other words, we can only hide our true self for so long before it slips into what we say. We can choose to use our words to advance the Lord's kingdom or defeat it. A lot of the defensiveness and negativity we put out into the world stems from the deep wounds inflicted on us by someone else's words.

I urge you to take a serious look into your habits and thoughts and find what is at the root of them. Attack the root and yank it up like a weed, tossing it into the garbage forever.

Also, be careful what you say to others and make sure your intentions are always pure. I felt that Lana was careless with the words she used towards me. She wasn't able to grasp the lasting effects her words would have on my life. We never know what someone else is going through, so it's better to be safe than sorry and show kindness and respect with what we speak.

Take the time to write down a list of the words that have been spoken to you, or that you may have spoken over others. Take a moment to ask God what He believes about you, and them. Write that down, too. You'll be surprised by the truths that come to mind. Pray those over yourself and over others whenever you have the chance.

Loving People

I won't dive too deeply into this one, as I elaborated on it earlier. However, to nail it on the head, it is so important to be selfless when loving someone and understand that everyone loves in a different way. We give and receive love in different languages—such as words of affirmation, quality time, acts of service, physical touch, and gifts. Having open conversations with the people around us or picking up on subtle cues in the way others act is crucial to developing healthy and well-balanced relationships.

Think about it in the context of my story. How much pain would I have been spared, how many fights avoided, if I had only learned this sooner? If you care about someone, you should want to learn about how they operate and show them that you appreciate them through putting in the effort to love them in their language and not just your own.

Sex

Oh, the things I've learned about this over the years. Sex is a topic we love talking about *so* much! Sex. The dirty word. The taboo topic that always needs more attention.

Before I go on, it's important for me to note that these insights are the result of what I have found through my own experience, growth, and faith. There is no shame and no condemnation here. Sex is a wonderful and beautiful act shared between two people. It's also incredibly gross, if you really think about it. I absolutely respect a difference of opinion, as well as people who choose to live their lives differently.

Did you know that the Bible only has two sets of relationship definitions? We are either brother and sister, or we are husband and wife. There's no in-between. That being said, would you treat your brother or sister that way? I sure hope not. We should treat our partner with that same respect until they are our husband or wife.

I think I could rest my case here, but I'll elaborate.

There are many passages throughout the Bible that command us to leave our father or mother and become one with our spouse. The act of sex binds us together into one flesh. We spiritually connect ourselves to another human being in a realm that's invisible to our human eyes. The severe way that society abuses the beauty and intimacy that sex was designed for, of which I have been guilty, is a sad perversion.

The chemicals emitted during a sexual encounter bind us together in addiction and blur our ability to properly evaluate the other person and our compatibility with them. A few years down the line, when the lustful sparks disappear, will we actually enjoy spending time together? Hanging out? Or will our relationships fizzle as we grow our separate ways? Adding sex into the equation before it has a rightful place is detrimental and disrespectful to ourselves and to God.

What might feel good in the moment is actually tearing you a step further away from yourself, from your future partner, and from God. This is where soul-ties come into play. We were designed to be bonded to one person, to marry one person, to have a family with one person. The more we tie ourselves to others, the harder it will be to fulfill God's purpose for relationship. The Bible is explicitly clear on this one.

If you knew me before Jesus, you may be reading this and laughing at my hypocrisy. But I promise you, the more I learn about this, the more I understand the severity of my past actions. Each breakup, each insecure thought, each relationship I had was negatively affected by the sexual encounters I had with each of the men in my life. Every single one. It's a lot easier to be a strong, independent, secure, and healthy person when you remove sex from the equation altogether. I can proudly assure you that no matter what your background, no matter what sin you may have committed, you are forgiven and born again through Jesus. You are new and you *can* start over! I have.

Make another list. Write down every person you've ever been with, dated, or crushed on. Take your time and pray through each name, breaking the chains, cutting the ties, and releasing your heart back to God. The freedom and power that comes from this activity is transformational. It may take more than one prayer. It may take one hundred prayers. Keep at it. You won't regret it.

Family

Family is blood. They birthed you, raised you, and love you in ways other people never will. But every family also has the potential to be harmful and toxic. I'm speaking directly to those who are struggling to fit in, step out, or just be honest with their family. Guess what? They aren't the end-all-be-all. Newsflash: once you turn of age, you are fully an adult capable of making your own decisions.

So I ask you, who cares? Who cares what someone else believes? Who decides what your truth is? Who decides what is right and wrong? If we could all spend less time judging and more time loving and accepting and knowing what we're running for, we could all live in peace. That's what family is meant to be.

My parents felt a lot of shame surrounding my decision to pursue Jesus. How could I walk away from my faith? What had they done wrong? They felt like they must have failed as parents. My communication with them dropped after I moved to Calgary. It took months before our conversations hit deeper than "How is work?" It took a full year after this story was written for our relationship to begin its mending process. There is much work to be done, but we are well on our way to moving forward.

Our new reality may never look like the old reality, but that's more than okay. We are evolving and growing and my relationship with my parents will forever be stronger for this. My dad and I now have something we both share an interest in and can talk about. Our faith may be different, but we share the same passion to learn and dive into the Torah and all that God laid out for our people. My mother and I have also been able to hit a deeper level, though it's a different dynamic than the one I have with my dad; we relate to the realities of life, relationships, and being out in the world and independent.

Fear not, when your problems seem hopeless, they are no match for God.

If you're walking through something similar, I feel for you and I'm praying for you. I hope my story brings you hope and peace surrounding your burdens. I thought my family was hopeless and that we would never recover, but it only took time.

The road to the future may have speedbumps, but my new outlook on life has opened doors to an entirely new level of relationship with my parents—and a lot of the groundwork for that comes from the person I have grown into and the grace and forgiveness I've worked on at my end.

The following verse provided a lot of comfort for me in regards to my family along the way. It illustrates the idea that you can say or feel what you want about Jesus, but unless the person you're talking to has personally encountered or experienced His love and mercy, they'll never understand. Only those with the Spirit can truly understand. It's our job to exemplify His grace and mercy on their behalf and do our best possible job to show the growth He endlessly provides for us. Have some grace for your family too:

> *The person without the Spirit does not accept the things that come from the Spirit of God but considers them foolishness, and cannot understand them because they are discerned only through the Spirit.*
> —I Corinthians 2:14

At times I see how my family handles a situation, talks about other people or reacts to something that's going on, and I wish they could rise above it. It makes me sad to know that I have the key to open a door to answers, inner peace, and endless love they're just not privy to.

So be patient. Don't rush them, but still put in the effort to connect.

Don't be afraid to pray it out. Pray for God to change their hearts and soften them. Find peace in knowing that we have the Spirit within us and rest in the additional family you'll create in your church. That's another reason why community is so important. At the end of the day, your family is your blood and they aren't going anywhere.

Faith vs. Religion

This is one of my favourite topics to discuss. There's a big difference between faith and religion. These terms often get misunderstood and misused.

Religion, to me, is an organized group—like, all of Christianity, or Judaism, etc. Religion is about going to synagogue or church because that's what you do, praying because you're supposed to, or observing only the cultural aspects of holidays. You only go through the motions.

The Tanach—the Hebrew Bible, what would be considered the Old Testament—and the New Testament are full of people who have intimate relationships with God, close encounters, and spiritual awakenings. People who are caught up in everyday "religion" have lost touch with those close encounters. Experience is the link between where religion ends and faith begins. Our supernatural out-of-body experiences are what tie us so tightly to our beliefs.

When we seek out God and experience Him on a daily basis, it's a whole new ball game. It tightens the knot, making permanent the understanding of why we do what we do out of love. Faith is the active belief in God, the active pursuit of Him, and living our lives accordingly. It's going to synagogue or church because we want to, because we value the time we spend there. We pray because it leads us deeper in connection with Him. When observing holiday traditions, we understand the deep meaning behind every action.

We can be Jewish and have no faith or we can be Christian and not actively pursue Jesus. To me, my faith isn't a religion. I often hesitate to even use the word *Christian*. I much prefer to say that I was raised Jewish and I follow Jesus now.

I have received a lot of criticism and eye-rolling for only listening to worship music, only reading books about Jesus, or only having Christian friends in Calgary. But what people fail to understand from the outside is that when you're running with Jesus, when you're actively pursuing Him in all that you do, you *want* to do all of those things. You *want* to talk about Jesus all the time, you *want* to spend your time praising Him through music and diving deeper into His words by growing the depth of your faith. Nothing else matters.

My story isn't about how I left Judaism to be a Christian; it's about me expanding my definition of faith to include the man who was sent to this earth to save me. The joy Jesus has brought into my life makes me want nothing other than to spend every waking moment falling more deeply in love with who He really is. There is no greater peace than that which comes from a life with Jesus.

Jesus is not a religion, He is a way of life.

I have told you these things, so that in me you may have peace. In this world you will have trouble. But take heart! I have overcome the world.
—John 16:33

God tells us that we will go through trouble and tribulations, but we will overcome because we're more than conquerors through Him (Romans 8:37). He calls us to suffer in order to succeed, and He promises that there is always beauty and growth in that process.

> Jesus is not a religion,
> He is a way of life.

Nothing in life comes easy, and sometimes the trials come, but we stand up and face them until we see through to the other side.

I've been fighting a battle with the enemy from the very second Jesus entered my life— whether it's in my mind, with my family, with men, or even financially. But here's the kicker: God has shown up time and time again. He has provided, reassured me, and stood by my side in protection.

> *For I am convinced that neither death nor life, neither angels nor de-*
> *mons, neither the present nor the future, nor any powers, neither height*
> *nor depth, nor anything else in all creation, will be able to separate us*
> *from the love of God that is in Christ Jesus our Lord.*
>
> —Romans 8:38–39

Sometimes I wonder where I would be if I had never met Chase, had Jesus introduced to me or created a home for me in Calgary. That thought isn't worth very much of my time because He had this plan for me all along. He saved me. Who the Son sets free is free indeed (John 8:36).

I no longer carry the burdens of my fears, rejection, and uncleanliness. God is a God of miracles. He can move mountains. He can break the chains and lift every curse. This is what freedom feels like, shedding my past and opening up the unknown and empty spaces deep within, allowing the Holy Spirit to fill me with His perfection. Nothing can compare. He has made me new and the best is yet to come!

> *But now apart from the law the righteousness of God has been made*
> *known, to which the Law and the Prophets testify. This righteousness*
> *is given through faith in Jesus Christ to all who believe. There is no*
> *difference between Jew and Gentile, for all have sinned and fall short*
> *of the glory of God, and all are justified freely by his grace through the*
> *redemption that came by Christ Jesus. God presented Christ as a sac-*
> *rifice of atonement, through the shedding of his blood—to be received*
> *by faith. He did this to demonstrate his righteousness, because in his*
> *forbearance he had left the sins committed beforehand unpunished—he*

did it to demonstrate his righteousness at the present time, so as to be just and the one who justifies those who have faith in Jesus. Where, then, is boasting? It is excluded. Because of what law? The law that requires works? No, because of the law that requires faith. For we maintain that a person is justified by faith apart from the works of the law. Or is God the God of Jews only? Is he not the God of Gentiles too? Yes, of Gentiles too, since there is only one God, who will justify the circumcised by faith and the uncircumcised through that same faith. Do we, then, nullify the law by this faith? Not at all! Rather, we uphold the law.

—Romans 3:21-31

Here are my final thoughts and questions to you. At the end of the day, who decides what is right for you? Who tells you what to believe? Who is in charge of your happiness?

Hint: It's you.